Life in
Twentieth Century America

The twentieth century is today, but it also was the "good old days" when woodburning was a family hobby, when a mother baked her own bread, and when Horatio Alger wrote 135 novels (or, as some critics charged, wrote one novel 135 times).

Professor Dodds tells how life was at the beginning of the century, and how it has evolved today. Since life today is reflected in current publications, the author devotes more attention to what was read, sung, laughed at, traveled on, and lived in by parents and grandparents, and it all makes for a lively social history.

LIFE

IN

TWENTIETH

CENTURY

AMERICA

By John W. Dodds

Edited by Louis B. Wright

CAPRICORN BOOKS EDITION
G. P. PUTNAM'S SONS NEW YORK

CAPRICORN BOOKS EDITION 1973

Copyright © 1965 by John W. Dodds
Revised edition Copyright © 1972 by John W. Dodds
All Rights Reserved

Published simultaneously in
Canada by Longman Canada Limited, Toronto
SBN: 399-50282-3
Library of Congress Catalog Card Number:
64–18036

PRINTED IN THE UNITED STATES OF AMERICA

Contents

LIFE IN  AMERICA

Edited by Louis B. Wright

Everyday Life In Colonial America
by Louis B. Wright

Everyday Life in Twentieth Century America
by John W. Dodds

Everyday Life in the Age of Enterprise
by Robert H. Walker

Everyday Life on the American Frontier
by Louis B. Wright

Everyday Life in the New Nation
by Louis B. Wright and Elaine Fowler

Life in
Twentieth Century America

Introduction

One of the interesting things about human nature is how people take for granted the everyday life that surrounds them. Older people can remember that things were "different" when they were young, and are sometimes inclined to moralize about how much better life seemed when it was simpler. Not many of them, however, would be willing to abolish jet airplanes in order to bring back the horse and buggy, to insist upon drawing water from a well rather than tapping into the municipal supply, or to bring back the good old days when the eleven-hour day was the accepted norm for labor. One must be careful not to confuse the idea of "civilization" with technological advance, but most of us accept with reasonable equanimity a way of life which would have astounded our great-grandfathers. It is easy to get used to luxuries which begin to seem like necessities, and to share the comfortable American belief that we have a downhill pull on Progress and that Progress will never end.

Suppose your twenty-first birthday had been January 1, 1901. What kind of world would you have wakened into, that first morning of the twentieth century? It would have depended somewhat upon who you were and where you happened to be living. Were you Annabella Lee Belmont, preparing to attend Mrs. Astor's fancy-dress ball at the Waldorf that night? Or (with a slight shift in gender) were you Steve Litvak, getting ready to enter the coal mines near Scranton, Pennsylvania? Or were you James McCutcheon, rising before dawn to milk the cows on a Nebraska farm? Obviously the various worlds these people inhabited were farther apart than the miles which separated them. Yet they had certain things, too, in common. In all likelihood none had seen the new toy which projected moving pictures on a screen, or had listened to Mr. Edison's other plaything, the phonograph, rasping out its approximation of the human voice. No one had heard the word "radio," for it hadn't been invented—the word or the instrument—though Mr. Marconi, later this same year, was to signal the letter "S" across the Atlantic from Cornwall, England, to Newfoundland. No one had even dreamed of television.

The highways, outside the cities, were dirt. "Superhighways" were not needed to accommodate the few mechanical gadgets known as automobiles which chugged haltingly around the countryside. No one had ever heard of a vacuum cleaner; people beat the dirt out of their carpets with wire whips. Electric lights were a fairly new gadget for well-to-do people in cities. Telephones were a luxury—and erratic; in 1900 there were only 20 per 1,000 of the population, as compared with 435 today. No one had ever flown in a lighter-than-air craft; the Wright brothers and Kitty Hawk were still two years away. "Astronaut" was a word that would not get into the dictionaries for half a century—outer space was left to the fantasies of Jules Verne's novels.

In this kind of U.S.A. what did people *do?* Did they have any fun? They thought so. And they worked, ate, went to bed and got up, had children and colds in the head and nursed toothaches and worried a little, sometimes, about life and death—just as people do today. These basic rhythms

10

of life do not change much from century to century. But Americans in 1901 were on the verge of an epoch which would bring incredible changes to the world they knew, and the daily lives of families from New York City to Medina, Ohio, to San Jose, California, would shift more rapidly than anyone could have believed possible.

This book will try to indicate some of the changes in that way of life. Much of it will have to do with the earlier part of the century, for it is there one meets the beginnings of so much that surrounds us today. But one must always keep today in mind as a point of reference, if only to sense the acceleration of changes which can be marked now in years instead of generations. Life since World War II and the atom bomb has given us a whole new set of achievements— and worries. We shall be concerned, however, with every-day things more than with the future of the human race; and there is a kind of reassurance in remembering the homely details of ordinary life, however amazing they are if we stop to think about them.

1

The Mobile American

WE have always thought of Americans as being a people on the move, contrasted with the more deeply rooted populations of Europe. And our pioneering past is not really so far away: a generation or two ago we were still exploring parts of our vast country and carving homesteads out of the wilderness. What we forget is that the people who moved our frontiers to the edge of the Great Plains and then to California and the western plains were a hardy but relatively small band. Settling the great reaches of the continent was the mission of a handful of people. Daniel Boone explained his restlessness by saying "I had to have elbow room." But the essential difficulties of transportation kept most people at home rather than on the road, even if they had dim urges to explore. They were accustomed to live out their lives in the county or even the neighborhood into which they were born, often without ever getting out of their home state. It took a lot of planning to get a horse and buggy a hundred miles.

The turn of the century *was* a horse-and-buggy era for America, town and country. In town, you either walked to your destination or took a horsecar (which you could do in some places as late as 1917), or perhaps one of those

BICYCLE FASHIONS
1905

Fashions for lady cyclists of 1905

newfangled electric trolleys which clanged and pounded their way through city streets. If you were lucky you could, in a city like San Francisco, combine transportation and excitement by roller-coasting over the hills in a cable car. Just as excitingly you could, where the pavements were not too rough, ride a bicycle. Americans, about 1900, were in the throes of a bicycle craze. There was a bicycle population of 10 million; 312 factories were making the machines, and between 1890 and 1896 over $100 million had been spent on "wheels." Cycling was romance as much as transportation—bicycle clubs were formed and young men and women breezed along side by side, or even on tandem wheels. Moralists and ministers took alarm; one of them warned: "You cannot serve God and skylark on a bicycle." On the

14

country roads, however, the less spectacular horse took over again. The mud and ruts were not for cyclists.

As America had moved westward, the growth of towns had followed the courses of the rivers, from the Susquehanna to the Allegheny to the Ohio to the Mississippi and points beyond, for the rivers were the channels of early mobility in the wilderness. By the twentieth century, however, the railroad had for some time been the accepted medium for longer travel. The breadth of the continent had been linked by rail as early as 1869. As the railway networks grew, linking city to city, new towns sprang up along the tracks and branch lines brought prosperity to towns hitherto buried in the landscape. Other towns, less happily situated, lost population and industry. The railroad meant wealth, mobility, communication, progress.

There are still many people alive who remember that one of the thrills of childhood was going down to the "depot" to watch the 10:25 pull in. Not infrequently it was on time. The huge pulsing engine—it seemed so gigantic— would slow to a screeching stop and stand there panting lazily while the blue-uniformed conductor looked at his big watch and the stream of passengers lucky enough to have

A railroading ad of the turn of the century

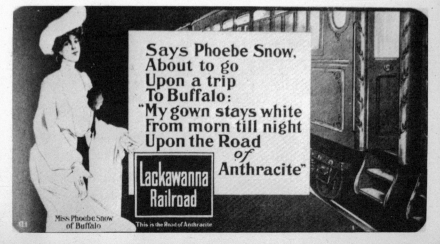

Says Phoebe Snow,
About to go
Upon a trip
To Buffalo:
"My gown stays white
From morn till night
Upon the Road
of
Anthracite"

Lackawanna
Railroad

Miss Phoebe Snow
of Buffalo

This is the Road of Anthracite

Though early motorists were taunted to "get a horse" when stuck in mud, even horses had their troubles.

had a train ride emerged from the splendid day coaches. Often one could catch a glimpse of the engineer, the master of this monster of steel, perched high above all ordinary folk. Shortly, on signal, the resting engine, its gleaming brass bell ringing, would snort quickly, ejecting puffs of black smoke. The mammoth wheels would begin to turn, and soon the 10:25 would disappear around the curve, to leave the station in sunny quiet until the arrival of the 3:27.

What boy today declares as his earliest ambition his hope to be a railroad engineer? What sight and sound today conveys the romantic nostalgia of a long, brightly lighted train gliding at night through the distant countryside, emitting not the short sharp barks of the diesel engine, but the long alluring lonesome notes of the steam whistle?

For many travelers the annual vacation trip to grandmother's, or to the lake (perhaps all of 150 miles away) was the event of the year. One was likely to choke in smoke and cinders but one loved it. The new electric railways which were connecting suburbia with the city and town with town weren't nearly as much fun. Interurban electric travel, with the cars reaching over rough roadbeds a swaying, window-rattling speed of 35 miles an hour, could be intimidating but never so deeply satisfying.

Aside from these mechanical marvels, however, transportation in the early century still belonged to the horse and buggy or the horse and wagon. The greater part of the United States was still in the mud. None but the lowly horse could negotiate the country roadways rutted in summer and quagmired in winter. Farmers went to town infrequently —to get grocery staples, to take grain to market, to pick up the weekly mail at the post office—for there was little Rural Free Delivery of mail in 1900; only 1,200 miles of such routes existed in the entire United States.

All this was to change, however, with what seemed like spectacular rapidity. There were 21 million horses and mules on farms in 1900; there were even some 14 million in 1940. By 1959 only 3 million were left, and then people seemed to stop counting. What had happened in between, of course, was the development of the internal-combustion engine, which changed the face of the nation and the way of life of a people.

The first motorized buggies, or motorcars (the word "automobile" didn't come into immediate use) were imports from Europe, owned mostly by those rich enough to afford such playthings. But their appeal to Yankee ingenuity was strong, and before long all kinds of backyard mechanics were building strange contraptions resembling buggies (even to the whipsockets), which spouted strange staccato noises and trembled into a kind of motion. For a number of years —until about 1908—the driver's seat was on the right, really the wrong side of the road for proper visibility, only

17

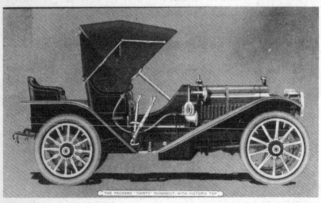

THE PACKARD "THIRTY" RUNABOUT WITH VICTORIA TOP

"Work while you work, play while you play"—the

OLDSMOBILE

Above, an Oldsmobile of 1902–1904. On the opposite page at the top is a 1905 Peerless, center is a 1910 Packard runabout, and at bottom a Pierce Arrow of 1906.

because that was the side on which the driver of the horse had always sat. These cars were chain-driven and were steered by a tiller rather than a wheel.

The first sale of an American gasoline car was made by the Duryea Motor Car Co. in 1896, in which year it built ten cars. By 1900 manufacturers had sprung up all over the place and over 4,000 Americans owned cars. The first automobile show, held at Madison Square Garden in 1900, had 31 exhibitors, eight of them showing electric and eight steam-driven cars. In one year, 1902, 55 new makes of cars appeared on the market; by 1909 there were 743 factories turning out motorcars. Over the years since 1900 there have been 2,726 manufacturers of autos in the United

19

States. Many of these cars lingered only experimentally for a year or two and then disappeared, but for some time the whole world of auto manufacturing was open to the ambitious entrepreneur. Even the Studebaker Carriage Company began to make automobiles, and one of the earliest successful steamers was put on the market by the White Sewing Machine Co.

In 1907, 43,000 cars were made; in 1908, 63,500; in 1920, 2 million, and in 1940, 3,717,385. By 1962 there were about 80 million motor vehicle registrations in the country, and in its best years, like 1964, the industry was turning out well over 8 million cars. These statistics are merely the cold statement of what amounted to a social revolution. They do not begin to capture the monumental thrill which the automobile brought to Americans in the first decades of the century.

Just to run through the names of some of the forgotten makes is to recall the glories of the past: Stutz Bearcat, Mercer Raceabout, Winton, Marmon, Peerless, Locomobile, Pierce-Arrow. If you read the old advertisements you discover that although the manufacturers were concerned with style and glamour, they assumed that the prospective purchaser was even more interested in stability and economy, and in detailed mechanical specifications. The Cameron Car people let you know that the body was built of "air-seasoned timber: oak sills and whitewood panels," that the bearings were of phosphor bronze and the lubrication was the "splash" system. The 1905 Buick ($950) announced an "actual 21 brake horsepower," and a "double cylinder opposed engine lengthwise within the frame." The "Velie 40" (there was a song written about it) was described in 1910 as having a "Brown-Lipe selective sliding gear, of 3½% nickel steel," and a "Splitdorf magneto, with non-vibrating coil."

Beauty and romance, however, were always just around the corner. One of the most famous ads in automotive history appeared in 1923 for a car called the Jordan Playboy.

Somewhere west of Laramie there's a broncho-busting steer-roping girl who knows what I'm talking about. She can tell what a sassy pony, that's a cross between greased lightning and the place where it hits, can do with eleven hundred pounds of steel and action that's going high, wide and handsome. The truth is—the Playboy was built for her. . . . She loves the cross of the wild and the tame. . . . Step into the Playboy when the hour grows dull with things gone dead and stale. Then start for the land of real living with the spirit of the lass who rides, lean and rangy, into the red horizon of a Wyoming twilight.

The ad sold cars.

In the beginning there was no standardization; even the interchangeable part was slow in arriving. No one make of auto looked like any other auto: you bought in each case a personality as well as a unique assemblage of machinery. You could invest $5,000 in a two-ton behemoth with as much as 40 horsepower, or you could buy, in 1907, a $500 Brush "runabout" with solid tires and a one-cylinder engine rated at 5 horsepower, which would run as fast as 25 miles an hour—if you could find roads to accommodate such speed. In between was a range of infinite variety. One of the arguments advanced against the heavier cars was that it took more than one horse to pull them out of the mud.

The most popular of the very early cars was the curved-dash "Merry" Oldsmobile, the first auto to reach anything like quantity production. In 1902 some 2,100 were sold, and in 1903, 3,750—one third of all the cars sold in the United States. It was a chain-driven, tiller-steered, 5-horsepower, 20-miles-per-hour job costing $650, and it represented breezy adventure for many Americans.

Mechanically, the early cars were a challenge to the patience and ingenuity of their owners. There were no self-starters or electric lights; the only illumination came from oil sidelamps and a pair of acetylene-gas headlights powered by a carbide generator which required delicate adjustment and frequent cleaning. Windshields were an extra, as was the huge toolbox with its complex array of indispensable wrenches, hammers, pliers, and vulcanizers—to say nothing of the towing cable. The pneumatic tires were precariously fragile. You expected them to blow out, and they did; the roadside wrenching of the tire off its "clincher" rim, the careful placing of the patch, and the wrestling of the tire back onto the rim were standard occupational hazards of motoring. A tire which ran as far as 3,000 miles was considered phenomenal.

You sat on high seats blown by the gusts of your 20-miles-per-hour speed, and if a sudden rain blew up, you and all the passengers fought to get the "one-man" folding canvas top into place—to say nothing of the isinglass side curtains. It took about fifteen minutes to accomplish this, and by that time you were wet anyway.

What was a motor trip like in 1908—say, out to Aunt Sarah's for the Fourth of July? The passengers bundled into the high seats of the massive four-cylinder Thomas Flyer. Normally, all were wrapped in linen dusters, and the men wore goggles and the women veils, for thick clouds of dust (impenetrable when you passed another car) were one of the conventions of motoring. After a rain you could take off the goggles, but you slipped and slithered on the greasy surface of the road, careening dangerously toward the ditches on the curves. You were lucky, in a way, if the mud was deep, for then your wheels could follow the wagon

An unusually clear photo of the 1903 Cadillac

ruts. But even this could lead to difficulties; if you met another vehicle you had difficulty twisting out of the deep grooves. If you got stuck in one of the bottomless mud puddles your only encouragement might come from small boys by the roadside, shouting "Get a horse!"

In 1962 the United States would spend $11,000,000,000 on highways, but in 1900 all the improved roads in the country, if laid end to end, wouldn't have reached from New York to Boston. As late as 1909 Pennsylvania had only 2,000 miles of improved road in its total of 100,000 miles. Even in 1921, when reasonably hardy people were crossing the continent, one-third of the highways that had to be negotiated between New York City and San Francisco were gravel or dirt. Some states, too, were frankly suspicious of this new competition for the horse. Missouri, in 1905, limited the speed of autos to nine miles per hour in every part of the state. According to the state law, each *county* could impose its own license fee of $2, and unless you had a string of licenses as long as your crank handle you made your way across the state at your own legal peril.

It was just as well, too, if you knew your way out to Aunt Sarah's. There were no road markers and very few signs, and the stranger had to depend pretty much on instinct.

But we don't really have the Thomas Flyer under way yet. After a delicate adjustment of the spark and gas levers on the steering column and perhaps the "priming" of the cylinders by pouring a little gasoline into petcocks fastened to the spark plugs, you heaved heavily on the crank. If everything was just right the motor "caught" with a series of spluttering gasps and you ran rapidly around to the driver's seat to adjust the levers to idling speed. By this time a kind of shattering rhythmic vibration was participated in by all the metal components of the car as well as by the passengers themselves. Then you kicked out the clutch, pushed the gear lever into the low-speed slot, released the clutch, and bounded away with a series of jackrabbit jerks. Your real mastery of this pulsating beast was next tested when you had to shift gears. A delicate touch was necessary to accomplish this intricate feat without a grinding and clashing which seemed sure to strip all the teeth off the gears.

You had a better than even chance of reaching your destination without mechanical calamity. Changing a tire was routine, but if you broke a spring you could only hope that you were near a blacksmith shop. If your gas got low you hunted the nearest livery stable, and the boy filled your

A two-mule-power solution for a muddy road

tank from a five-gallon can with a chamois strainer to keep
out water. If you needed water, however, for your radiator,
you kept looking ahead for the next watering trough by
the roadside. Nothing was more common than to see cars
immobilized, belching steam like a railway locomotive.

When you met a nervous horse (and it was surprising
how many horses were nervous) state laws often required
that you come to a dead stop while the angry driver led
his horse past. And timid people who disliked the whole

Sometimes there was a long wait for assistance

91022

idea of motorized transportation complained about the clatter of the auto as it approached and the rich ripe oily smell that lay heavy in the atmosphere after it had gone by. Municipal laws often limited your speed, within city limits, to five or ten miles per hour. On the open road speed limits were usually twenty miles per hour—and fast enough, too, unless you wanted to shake your liver loose.

This was motoring in the days when cars were cars and not merely automatic mechanisms. It was not yet quite everyday life in America, but it was on its way.

A whole romantic literature sprang up around the automobile, and songs were written celebrating the delights of the road. "My Merry Oldsmobile" was the best known of these, though "Get Out and Get Under" had more meaning for most motorists. "Love in an Automobile" (surprisingly modern) appeared in 1899, and "Take Me Out for a Joy Ride" in 1909. In 1928, when Henry Ford introduced his Model-A car, Walter O'Keefe wrote a song called "Henry's Made a Lady Out of Lizzie." But by 1928 the history of the earlier Model-T had been written indelibly into the contours of the American countryside, and into the American heart.

Probably no one man had more effect on the daily lives of most Americans than did Henry Ford. In the early part of the century the delights of motoring had not been for the many; it was an expensive pastime. Good roads would be necessary if the farmer were to be lifted out of the mud, but in the meantime what was needed was a cheap, sturdy, simple car that could get the traveler *through* the morasses. Ford gave the answer in 1908 with his Model-T, which influenced not merely ways of life but the whole system of industrial production. Ford pioneered the assembly line. He paid men the incredible wages of five dollars a day to put cars together as they went by on moving lines. By 1914,

26

Both the song and the car are still popular.

one hour and 33 minutes of a man's time would assemble a chassis—a revolution in mass production.

The car which emerged from this process was probably the best-loved car ever made. In 1908 it cost $850, but by 1917 it was $360, and in 1925 one model sold for $290. This was stripped down, of course; when you bought a Ford it was only a point of departure. Its color was always

This advertisement in the *Saturday Evening Post* in 1908 heralded the first appearance of the Model-T.

black. It had no bumpers, no speedometer, no rearview mirror (why would you want to see what was coming from behind?); no accelerator, no temperature indicator (you could always tell when the engine boiled); no spare tire. Shortly after purchase, you began to order from the Sears, Roebuck catalog the accessories which were to adorn simplicity and make it comfortable: shock absorbers, an accelerator, a decorative radiator cap, clips to keep the brake rods from rattling, gas gauges, bigger rear brakes, an oil gauge—even splash-proof flower vases if yours was an enclosed model.

This 1914 photograph shows Ford bodies being positioned onto chassis. The moving assembly line was introduced by Henry Ford in 1913.

The Ford was meant for service, and no fooling about it. You bought a left-hand drive (shortly all other manufacturers followed suit), and 22 horsepower capable of 35 miles an hour if you dared let it go. It had a "planetary" if not exactly astronautic transmission. It was an ungainly beast, seven feet high with its top up, and it had its eccentricities—just like a horse. You learned to know its whimsies and even to love them as individualities, just as you would love a likable though temperamental member of the family. Basically, however, the Ford was as dependable as it was simple. If it got out of shape you bent it back; if something sagged, you fixed it with baling wire. If the radiator leaked you fed it bran, just as you would feed a horse—and somehow, inexplicably, the bran stopped the leak (sometimes) without clogging the engine. Most things could be fixed by direct action.

Driving the Ford was simplicity itself. Once you had cranked it and had leaped into the driver's seat over the left-hand side of the tonneau (there was no left-hand door), you merely advanced the throttle, pushed your foot down authoritatively on the low-speed pedal, and were off with an instant acceleration. At about eight miles an hour you let the pedal fall back into high gear, and with a sudden jerk you were bouncing on your way. The high road clearance of the car was designed for rough and muddy country highways. Its three-point suspension made it as lithe and flexible as a cat.

Ford design was a triumph of consistency—it never changed basically. Henry Ford had sold 15 million Tin Lizzies, as they were fondly called, before he was forced by competition to introduce, grudgingly, the new Model-A in 1928. Between 1917 and 1927 one-half of the cars produced in the United States were Fords. There are still some

The first Model-T Ford

FORD MOTOR COMPANY

on the highways; in 1963 Sears, Roebuck still listed valves, motor gaskets, and front-wheel bearings for the Model-T.

Everybody made affectionate fun of the car and bought Ford jokebooks. Long after most Model-T's had gone to the junkyard there remained a few faithful owners. As late as 1953 a man was fined in San Francisco for speeding in a Model-T. His courtroom comment was: "She was only hittin' on three; if she'd been hittin' on all four I doubt if they would have caught me."

The day was coming fast when almost every American would ride on rubber. Better roads made it possible for more cars to go farther, faster. In 1908 there were fewer than 200,000 motor vehicles in a nation of 90 million people; by 1940, even after the depression years, 32 million; by 1962, about 80 million. First came the macadam road, then the concrete highway, then the superhighway— all of them clotted today with the cars without which our population would be immobilized, and *with* which, in traffic, it is often immobilized anyway, or still worse, slaughtered. In 1915, 5,800 people were killed in motor accidents; in 1963, 43,000 died on the highways. There is a curious hidden fact here, however. The deaths in 1963 were in the ratio of 5 per 10,000 cars; in 1915, 24 per 10,000 cars. One lived proportionately more dangerously on the roads then than now!

Not only has the automobile become essential to the daily locomotion of millions of people, it has also become the backbone of the economy. It is said that today 10 million Americans are "directly or indirectly employed in the manufacture, sale, or maintenance of automobiles." Scores of subsidiary industries—glass, copper, steel, aluminum, rubber, gasoline and oil—depend on the welfare of Detroit for their existence. Autos consume one-fifth of the nation's steel, three-fifths of its rubber, nearly half the lead, and a

31

major portion of the aluminum, glass, zinc, and nickel. Motor courts and restaurants have been spawned by the thousands to accommodate the traveler. If John Doe doesn't buy that new car next year millions of people may be out of work!

The rise of the automobile saw also the decline of the railway as a means of travel. As late as 1930 there were 430,000 miles of track in operation; by 1962, only 376,000 miles. In 1930 passengers were carried by rail 708 million miles; in 1962, 313 million. And the disappearance of electric railways, both urban and interurban, has been even more marked. In 1935 there were 26,700 miles of electric railway in operation; in 1962 about 2,500 miles. One of the ironies of present-day progress is that there is much talk about the revival of interurban and suburban electric transport, simply to reduce the incredible congestion of the highways and parking lots.

These ironies are evident also in the development and even more in the mutation of the auto trailer as a means of transportation. It was just beginning to come into popular use about 1940 and served as a means to get families out on the road for long trips in self-sufficient surroundings. Since the war the trailer business has boomed; in 1963 over 72,000 travel-trailers were built, an increase of 15,000 over the previous year. In the same year 150,000 "mobile homes" were sold. Today some 4 million Americans live in house trailers—and the important word there is "live." From smallish, cramped approximations of living space, trailers have grown into 30-to-50-foot monsters of the highway. But the large ones are seldom seen on the highways; they have to be hauled by trucks to "trailer courts" (of which there are some 16,000 in the U. S.) where they are planted semipermanently, decorated by window flower boxes and little white picket fences. Again the mobile has become the immobile. Their inhabitants love them because of the paradoxical sense of freedom they get from household cares in such confined space. Life in the house trailer has become one of the patterns of American civilization.

What has been the effect of our accelerated mobility on the total structure of American life? There is hardly any aspect of that life it has not influenced.

For one thing, the old restlessness of the pioneer seems to have entered the American bloodstream again. The deep-rootedness of families in the early nineteen-hundreds, when the man who moved to the next county often found himself a stranger, has been disappearing. People *are* on the move. If they retire they are as likely to sell the old house and go to California or Florida or Arizona as to dwindle away in the home town. New business opportunities transplant other people across the country. Industries, with far-flung branches and subsidiaries, often move their employees as if they were chessmen. A statistic or two points this up: From March, 1961, to March, 1962, nearly 5.5 million people moved to a different county in their home state, and over 5.5 million to a different state.

The long ribbons of highway have tended to homogenize the U.S.A. Oklahoma is still different from New Hampshire, but there are hundreds of towns across the country in which, if you were taken there blindfolded, you would think yourself at home, for they are strikingly similar. Their news-papers are equally bad, or good; the stop-and-go signs are identical; the streets are equally congested with the same carbon-copy cars and the parking is equally difficult. The same packaged foods appear on the shelves of the same chain stores. The same kinds of builders' developments

With Orville at the controls, the Wright brothers' plane rises for its historic flight on December 17, 1903.

fringe the towns. In the same kind of motel you can see the same television program that is being watched by 40 million other people.

Even if you are not on the move, your family life is vastly different from that of 1900. There are many reasons for this, but we are still thinking of the automobile. It is true that family tensions have been known to develop over the question: "Who will have the car tonight?" But even in 1940 Junior was likely to have his own jalopy. He is almost sure to have it today, and if he takes his girl to the drive-in movie (that strangely modern conjunction of technologies) the parents can either be happy that he has entertainment or can worry about what might happen on the highway coming home. But the automobile has done as much to consolidate family life as to disrupt it. The station wagon has often become the family car, into which the whole spectrum of young and old clamber to take off for the mountains or lake or seashore—or just the local picnic grounds. More families see more parts of the country than ever before in history; each summer increased numbers of out-of-state licenses pass down Main Street. People are seeing America first. If one had to choose a single symbol to represent daily

Charles Lindbergh and his *Spirit of St. Louis*

life in the United States now, it would be the horseless carriage.

Of course not all mobility today hinges on the automobile. Americans are flooding Europe each summer. One wonders what one's grandfather would have said in 1900 if he had been told that in 1963 people would fly from New York to London or Paris in six and a half hours for $200. He would have snorted, of course. One wonders if even the Wright brothers would have envisioned it in 1903 at Kitty Hawk when the first successful flying machine lifted Orville Wright off the ground and flew for twelve seconds—or even

DOUGLAS AIRCRAFT CO.

The DC-3, early workhorse of commercial airlines

six years later, when Louis Blériot flew all 17 miles of the English Channel for the first time in his 25-horsepower monoplane. Or the next year, 1910, when one Walter Brookins won a $10,000 prize for flying a Wright biplane from Chicago to Springfield, Illinois, a distance of 187 miles.

Although airplane travel is not exactly a daily way of life for most people today, it has become very much a part of the American consciousness. It was a pioneer if relatively unimportant weapon of World War I, and the determining factor in World War II. Between the wars, when it was just coming of age, the airplane caught the public imagination as few other things had.

This was particularly true during those incredibly thrilling days of 1927 when a young man of twenty-five was flying his single-engine plane, solo, across the wastes of the Atlantic Ocean. A whole nation hung on the event, and

The DC-8, modern transcontinental and transoceanic jet

when Charles Lindbergh landed safely at Paris the pride and relief of his countrymen were almost tangible things. There is no need to retell the well-known story here, but if you were looking for heroes in American life Lindbergh would have qualified, in the minds of many, along with Washington and Lincoln. At the very least it was a real "first," and Americans, in more recent years, have grown accustomed to having fewer such aerial firsts.

Pan American began its first passenger service to Europe in 1929. In 1930 the first "all-air" transcontinental passenger flight was made, by the Ford Tri-Motor plane, affectionately called the "Tin Goose." It left Los Angeles at dawn and arrived at Newark, N. J., the next afternoon. In 1931 Wiley Post and Howard Gatty flew around the world in eight days and fifteen hours.

But even by 1940, thirteen years after Lindbergh, commercial airplane transportation was efficient but still in its infancy—this despite the fact that there were 2,300 airports, of one kind or another, in operation, and that scheduled domestic air carriers flew 1,052,000,000 air passenger-miles. Since then the airplane has shrunk the United States to almost postage-stamp size. In 1963 there were 3,451 public airports into which flew scheduled planes carrying people 50,000,000,000 passenger-miles. Private flying has also grown to astounding proportions. In 1940 there were 50,000 certified private pilots. Today there are more than ten times that many, flying business and pleasure aircraft nearly 2,000,000,000 miles a year.

Nothing we shall see in the following chapters will describe a more fundamental shift in daily life in the twentieth century than this picture of transportation. Although our total civilization is not, happily, to be equated with the internal combustion or the jet engine, our new mobility has changed the shape and nature of farms and towns and cities, of business and manufactures, of work and leisure—indeed of health and illness, if automotive smog is the growing hazard it seems to be! The problem of whether or not most of us are happier because we can go more places faster need not be discussed here. We're on our way, and we'd better like it. Tomorrow the moon!

2

Town and Country: Varieties
of Everyday Life

LIFE on the farm in the first year of the twentieth century was more like 1860 than 1940. In the first place, the majority of the people lived there. The population of the United States in 1901 was 77,585,000, and of this 60 percent was rural. The rhythms of daily life, set by the sun, had changed very little over the years, whether in the larger spaces of the great plains or on the smaller farms of the East and South. Horsepower and manpower were still the units of energy for the spring planting of the crops, the summer cultivating, the autumn harvesting, and for a multitude of other daily duties. Some reaping of grain was still done by hand with the scythe or "cradle," though the horse-drawn McCormick reaper had changed all this in most communities.

The cows were milked by hand and the milk was put in large pans and placed in a cool structure. Sometimes the structure was called a "milk house," but if it could be located over or alongside a spring it was a "springhouse." There the cream would rise to the surface to be skimmed and churned—for all farmers made their own butter, or rather their wives and children did. Sometimes the more mechanically minded had a "dogpower" churn, turned by a set of gears activated by a dog walking on a treadmill. Farm families baked their own bread and of course raised their own fruits and vegetables and slaughtered their own meat. The occasional Saturday trips to the nearest general store were to get such staples as flour, navy beans (white kidney beans), molasses, oatmeal, and for the winter diet, dried prunes or peaches. And sometimes, for the children, candy—"jawbreakers," or long beltlike strips of licorice. Farmers had to be largely self-sufficient. Even as late as 1955 they had an average annual family income, from the farms themselves, of less than $1,000. In 1900 it would have been less than half of that.

People on the farms, then, lived much like their fathers and grandfathers before them. They rose before dawn most of the year and went to bed at night by kerosene lights and cooked their meals on wood or coal stoves. Even by 1935 only one farm home in ten was wired for electricity. There was no plumbing; they drew water from springs or wells, bathed in a washtub in the kitchen, and made treks to an outhouse which could hardly be called a sanitary "convenience." The roads connecting the scattered villages and farms were drifted with snow in the winter, bogged with mud in the spring, and deep with dust in the summer. Children walked to the one-room country schoolhouse (of which there were still 150,000 in 1930), where the teacher, if she represented the national norm, received an annual salary of $325.

Children had their own delights, of course: picking chestnuts or hunting in the woods on crisp October mornings, fishing and swimming in nearby "cricks," gathering wild blackberries or blueberries, finding the first trailing arbutus under the snow in the early spring, listening to sleigh bells on a tingling winter night.

Any community activity was largely a neighborhood one:

Steam threshing in 1906

picking up the rare mail and the weekly paper at the village post office (farmers were not given to extensive correspondence); talking politics across the line fence with a neighbor; getting dressed up in store clothes to go to the rural Sunday school and church services. The local minister often had two parishes some miles apart, and often he did some farming during the week. Sometimes there were Sunday school picnics or "strawberry festivals" in the churchyard or evening "socials" at the schoolhouse, with orations, selected literary readings and even debates—both children and parents nodding sleepily in the hot little schoolroom after a hard day's work. There was a good deal of "neighboring" when larger tasks required joint effort, such as the raising of a rooftree for a new barn. At harvest time steam threshing machines made the rounds from farm to farm and "thrashing day," with the women preparing gargantuan meals for the hungry farmers, was always a great community event.

Occasionally families enjoyed something in the nature of a celebration. Sometimes a one-ring circus would visit

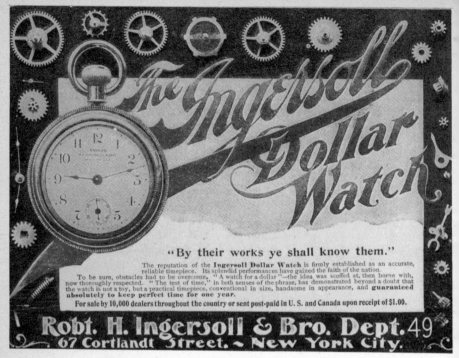

Advertisement for the famous Ingersoll watch, 1901

the county seat, and everyone would pile into a wagon (or even at times take the "hack" that ran between towns) for a day's outing. The annual county fair was a great event, too—an exciting mélange of horse-cattle-pig exhibitions, prize-winning pies and canned fruits and vegetables, horse races, lots of popcorn and soda pop, and a sort of carnival sideshow which parents inspected critically before allowing the children to attend.

Pleasures were for the most part simple, and the life very close to the soil. People talk today about getting back to the land. Most of them have little idea of what it meant to be on the land in 1900, the really hard life it represented.

As the twentieth century wore on, the story of farm life became in part a story of flight to the towns. More and more children were reluctant to commit themselves to the lives their fathers lived, though town existence for many of them, in mill or factory, was even more precarious. But the small farm had become progressively a less and less profitable economic unit. Elaborately mechanized machinery made possible the mass production of crops but also required larger investments; thus farms became consolidated into larger acreages in fewer hands. By 1940, 55 percent of the population of the United States was urban, 45 percent rural. By 1960 the figure of 1900 had almost exactly reversed itself: 63 percent was urban, 37 percent rural. Indeed the proportions were even more disparate than this census figure indicates, for "rural" by definition included towns of under 2,500. In 1961 the actual farm population, which as late as 1920 was about 32 million (30 percent of the population) had declined to under 15 million. The number of farms had been more than cut in half. Even between 1940 and 1962 the percentage of the nation's total work force on farms had decreased from 20 percent to 7 percent.

And as for those who continued to live on farms, life moved into the twentieth century as we think of it. The tractor replaced the horse; big combines reaped and threshed the grain simultaneously; electricity revolutionized domestic ways of life; bathrooms appeared in most farmhouses, and the Sears, Roebuck catalogs opened new vistas of technological comfort. The one-room schoolhouse became vestigial; although the total population increased by 56 million between 1930 and 1960, such schoolhouses decreased from 150,000 to 20,000. School buses now took country children to consolidated district grade schools and high schools. Most important of all, improved highways got the farmer out of the mud and into an automobile, and the nearest sizable town was now quickly accessible for shopping and entertainment. The farmer's daughter wore clothes like her city sister's and attendance at the latest movie was a possibility for the whole family.

Underwear ad, 1905

In many cases the newer suburbs reached out into the far countryside. Today the farmer who rolls along the superhighway doesn't even need to go to town to find an elaborate shopping center. Thus even as the agricultural population shrank, what was left of it became more like the rest. Radio, and later television, gave access, for better or worse, to the same world that everyone else knew. No one who flies across the country today can fail to be impressed by the miles upon miles of open countryside and the spreading fields. But no longer do the owners of those fields live in a different kind of culture.

If the rhythms of farm life in the early nineteen hundreds were different from today, those of urban life were even more different. Nearly half of all the people in towns and cities were in places of under 10,000. The small town was in many ways the heart of America. It has been written about, sung about, satirized, dramatized, and has become the symbol (sometimes even the sentimentalization) of the American way of life half a century ago. The cities were growing, burgeoning—frequently with people who were

44

fleeing the farms, and they in turn were becoming the focus of the new industrialization which was the hallmark of the U.S.A. But the industrial cities were still strange conglomerate masses of people, more and more foreign as they became swollen, after the 1870's, with the floods of immigrants from central and southern Europe who were manning the factories and mills. In 1895 nearly half of the population of such cities as New York and Chicago were first-generation immigrants. The great continuities of the American tradition could be more easily identified in the smaller towns.

Life moved slowly in these places, and before World War I changes came slowly, too. To be sure, new motorcars came to town and snorted, smoky and smelly, up and down the brick or cobblestone streets. Many homes had gas, though not yet electricity, and except for the poorer districts, bathrooms and plumbing. Central heating was still something of a luxury; coal or gas stoves kept people warm, and many who were youngsters then can still remember the beautiful frost crystals inside the windowpanes on cold winter mornings. There were other remembered things, too: the rich smell of buckwheat cakes that came up the back stairs early in the morning; cutting and dragging in the tall Christmas tree from the nearest woods through the December snow and decking it with strings of popcorn and tinsel and puffs of white cotton; the long winter evenings when children did their homework around the dining-room table while mother darned socks and long black cotton stockings and father read the paper under the fishtail gaslight—or perhaps under a glaring Welsbach gas mantle which flooded the whole room with hissing brilliance.

No one thought of life then as being "stylized," but it was eminently predictable and its patterns rested upon a comfortable recurrence. Monday was always washday; Tuesday ironing day; Wednesday baking day; Friday cleaning day, and so on. Not infrequently the big sprawling kitchen was the center of much of the family life. People not only ate many of their meals there, but small children played there under the mother's eye. It was a kind of all-purpose room which architects and families of the later mid-century were to rediscover with delight.

Houses were set well back on roomy lots with lots of trees for youngsters to climb and with room for a sizable vegetable garden. Each house had its front porch where on summer evenings the adults would sit in porch swings and hold long conversations with friends and neighbors who came over to "visit." Everybody knew everybody else in the early-century American town; most of the families had lived there all their lives. The doctor was your friend as well as your physician. You knew the grocer and the dry-goods store owner and the schoolteacher, as well as the plumber and the carpenter—each of whom, incidentally, took pride in being a *good* plumber and a *good* carpenter. They shared the hymnbook with you in church and it never entered their heads that they weren't just as dignified—in the sight of man as well as in the sight of God—as anyone else.

The American small-town Sunday was really a day of rest then, for the codes in many places were such that almost any non-pious activity was frowned on. It was not a day for picnics, sports, or frolic, or even for reading that was not edifying. Father might take a long afternoon snooze, but the children, before they were released to read *The Youth's Companion,* might well have to study the *Shorter Catechism* and read a chapter in Wayland's *Elements of Moral Science.* Some towns took pride in having persuaded the railroad not to run local trains on Sunday, and others even banished the Sunday papers from the newsstands. The

FALL SUITS

MADE TO ORDER $6 to $25

The new Fall styles are entirely different from last season's models.

Our Style Book illustrates what will be most fashionable in New York this season, including both long and short coat effects — over **150** designs from which to select.

Our samples show the newest fabrics. Your choice of over **400** materials which we carry in stock, every one thoroughly shrunken, fast colors and guaranteed to give good service.

STYLE BOOK AND SAMPLES SENT FREE

We keep no ready-made goods. Every garment is made to order, so that it will fit and become the one woman for whom it is intended.

We have fitted over **375,000** women by mail. That is why we know we can fit you.

We take the risk, as we will refund your money if we fail to fit you — you to be the judge.

No matter where you live, we have customers in your section to whom we can refer as to the success and honesty of our methods.

There is no guess-work or experimenting about our perfect-fitting system. Our simple measurement directions make it easy for you to order from us by mail. What we have done for thousands of others, we certainly can do for you.

Our Style Book explains how we can fit you by mail, and illustrates:

Visiting Costumes - - -	$6.00 to $20
Tailor-Made Suits - - -	$7.50 to $25
New Fall Skirts - - -	$3.50 to $12
Rain Coats - - - -	$9.75 to $20
Jackets and Coats - -	$5.75 to $25

We prepay express charges to any part of the U. S.

We Send Free by return mail to any part of the United States our new **Fall and Winter Style Book** showing the latest New York Fashions, a large assortment of samples of the newest materials, and simple directions for taking measurements correctly. **Write for them to-day.** Kindly state whether you wish samples for a suit, skirt, cloak or rain coat and about the colors you desire, and we will send a full line of exactly what you wish.

NATIONAL CLOAK AND SUIT CO.

The well-suited lady of autumn, 1905

Puritan Ethic made Sunday something to be endured even for those who did not question its premises. But no one returned to work Monday morning tired out!

Some of the best reading for one who wants to capture

A dapper 1909 gentleman

the tangibilities of life as it was lived in country and town during the first third of the century is in the pages of the Sears, Roebuck catalogs. Here is the record of what people actually bought and used, from farm machinery to clothes to books to household equipment—bought at a price which seems fantastically low today. At the turn of the century you could get oak well buckets for 36 cents each, potbelly stoves at $2.40, wood-or-coal kitchen ranges for $7.00; five-pound tubs of apple butter for 40 cents, maple syrup for 67 cents a five-gallon jug. A 30-volume set of the *Encyclopaedia Britannica* sold for $29.50. (It was true, of course, that the average hourly wage in industry was 29 cents. Farm laborers received a dollar a day.)

From the 1905 catalog people bought patent medicines, for example, guaranteed to cure almost any ailment flesh is heir to—or tombstones, if they felt themselves beyond the reach of medicine. They bought perfumes (Hyacinth, Crab-Apple, White Heliotrope, New Mown Hay, Shandon Bells, Ylang Ylang) for about 25 cents an ounce, and even rouge of a kind, "Rouge de Theatre," as well as hair bleach. Soap, however, did not yet pretend to do anything for you but make you clean. But by 1935 beauty aids filled ten pages of the catalog: Max Factor, Coty, Hudnut, and Harriet Hubbard Ayer had come on the scene; and even the farm ladies were taught the merits of lipstick, eyelash mascaras and curlers, eyebrow pencils, wrinkle creams, deodorants.

The American woman was continually being refashioned. In 1905 Sears offered 150 models of "shirtwaists," all of which had ceased to be fashionable before World War I. Long dust-dragging skirts changed into slit skirts and hobble skirts in 1913. They got shorter in the twenties—above the knee by 1926—then longer, then shorter, then longer. . . . The big hats in the 1905 catalog ("dressy" and "nobby"), topped with massive feathers and speared with hatpins, shrank to the cloche hats of the twenties, and then came back as high style in the sixties. Plumes, however, were out by 1925.

The heavily corseted wasp waist of 1905 ("Straight Front Fine Batiste Corset, Bias Gored, at 50 cents"), always under attack by doctors and Anti-Lacing Societies, had relaxed, by the time of World War I, into more natural contours—to be girded up again, as styles changed and technology improved, by the new elastic girdles. The cotton and lisle stockings of 1905 gave way to silk and rayon. By 1930, 300 million pairs of silk stockings were being sold each year, and milady and the girl in the five-and-ten-cent store began to look alike.

The man of the house could buy a natty, nifty suit right out of the Sears, Roebuck pages in 1905 for $15 (the top price, unless he wanted to send in his measurements for a semi-custom suit for which he might have to pay $25). It was always worn over long underwear in chilly seasons. His shirts did not button but were pulled on over the head. His collars were detachable and always stiffly starched (unless they were celluloid). Not until years later would the high stiff collar be replaced by the soft attached collar. He

49

Men's collar styles change slowly. From left to right, the Arrow collar of 1905, 1910, 1914, and 1925.

wore high shoes—sometimes button shoes for stylishness—and went to bed in a nightshirt. If he journeyed to the seashore he wore a bathing suit almost as all-enveloping as his wife's, and almost as hazardous if he chose to swim.

But if the man of 1905 went hunting, he had 14 pages of shotguns to choose from in the catalog. If his wife needed a stove or kitchen range (wood, coal, coke, gas, or kerosene) there were 30 pages displaying such basic equipment. To go with the stove were copper washboilers, galvanized tubs, hand-operated wringers, flatirons weighing four or five pounds, and even a hand-wheel-operated washing machine, if she had $5.10 to spend.

Early-century life in the American town was without much artistic or cultural pretension; there was little to excite the intellect. Women were the accepted guardians of such arts as existed, from china painting to woodburning to attendance at a monthly "literary" society. Nor was the life

he BELMONT & the CHESTER are
he new

ARROW
COLLARS

ith the notch that makes them
t perfectly.   15¢ 2 for 25¢

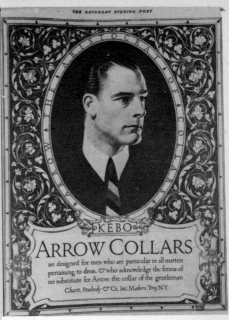

entirely idyllic either in work or pleasure: gossip, mean-
ness, selfishness, and arrogance were not unknown, for
Americans were still part of the human race. Sinclair Lewis
in 1920 satirized the sterility and drabness of the "Gopher
Prairies" across the country in *Main Street*. Small-town
America was pretty well isolated from the larger streams of
sophistication and world knowledge. It moved in the regular
channels of its own insularity, taking its politics, perhaps,
more seriously than today, but able to see the world in comfortable terms of black and white, with no apprehension
that before long Europe would reach out to involve the
United States in a war which would shatter all such insulari-
ties forever. Paris was light-years away from the ordinary
American of 1914. But shortly the doughboys would be
singing "How ya gonna keep 'em down on the farm, after
they've seen Paree—ee?"

The age of security was about over. Until then, however,

with all its slowness, inconvenience, and monotony, and with all its frequent economic hardship, life was wrapped in a kind of warm certainty—in part, perhaps, because it centered so much in the home, the very routines of which gave unity to daily life. People believed in themselves, in their town, in their civilization.

In describing this life, and its breakup, in his reminiscent book *The Age of Confidence,* Henry S. Canby said:

> We had been trained to fit into certainties, educated to suppose that Mr. Carnegie's steel mills, Sunday observance, the banking system, the Republican party, the benefits of Latin, algebra, and good handwriting . . . were parts of one quite comprehensible plan. We had no more attempted to relate industrial concentration with politics, or our distrust of art with the profit-making motive, than we had tried or been taught to discover a possible connection between Caesar and chemistry, or the Golden Rule and American history. Hence when acceleration began, for most of us about 1910, we were cleft. . . . Yet whispering at the back of the new liberal mind was always a question which became more insistent as the years went on. The community in which we had been brought up and the education ground into us were ordered, self-contained, comprehensible, while this new society was incoherent, without fixed aim, and without even a pretense of homogeneity. We were like pond fish who had been flooded into a river.

As the century progressed the disruptive influences became the everyday ones. Just as the country came closer to the town, the town lost its unique set of identities and became a part of a larger national complex. The same set of revolutionary influences was at work: the automobile, which put the family on wheels and sent its members, frequently, in different directions; radio and television, which brought the same world into everyone's living room; the growth of available power and electricity which made available to both city and town the same appliances and gadgets, and across the country the same neon lights illuminating the same drugstores and motels and gas stations.

Improvements in education brought to almost every town its respectably well-stocked library and sent increasing numbers of high school graduates on to colleges and universities. In 1900 there were only 238,000 students attending institutions of higher learning. In 1965, it is estimated, there will be 5.4 million, and by 1970, 7 million. In 1900 there were about 27,000 students graduated from our colleges; in 1960, 392,400. Along with this came an increased cultural awareness. Many towns developed museums of one kind or another, and brought in a winter lyceum series of lectures and music.

From the early nineteen-hundreds into the mid-twenties the institution of Tent Chautauqua served as an agency of culture as well as entertainment for millions—a six-day amalgam of uplift and education and fun. Many Americans a little past middle age can remember sitting in a sweltering tent in August and listening to the Swiss Bell Ringers or the Bohemian Band, or even, if they were fortunate, to Madame Ernestine Schumann-Heink. Many people watched their first primitive movies in a Chautauqua tent, and others saw their first Shakespeare when the Ben Greet Players came to town. Many famous people took to the Chautauqua circuit—humorists like Irvin S. Cobb or Stephen Leacock; crusaders like Judge Ben Lindsey or Clarence Darrow; public figures like Herbert Hoover, Walter Lippmann, Woodrow Wilson, and Al Smith. From 1904 on William Jennings Bryan gave the same speech, "The Prince of Peace," 3,000 times for Chautauqua. The only man to get

Season ticket holders at Tent Chautauqua

more mileage out of a single speech was Dr. Russell H. Conwell, a preacher and another Chautauqua trouper. He delivered his "Acres of Diamonds," a two-hour lecture, to 6,000 audiences, and never seemed to tire of it himself. People could take their oratory straight in those days!

By 1924 the multiple Chautauqua circuits (there were a hundred by that time) were reaching 30 million people in 12,000 towns. Tents were pitched that summer in 500 towns in Iowa alone. Tent Chautauqua went under about 1930, a casualty of the growth of mass media of communication and entertainment, and possibly of the economic depression of the 1930's. But with all its deficiencies and limitations, Tent Chautauqua brought a kind of enlightenment to vast segments of the American people and was an important index of smalltown American taste and culture in the first quarter of the century. It was as American as ice cream and the Fourth of July.

Greater forces, however, were breaking down the isolation of the United States. Two World Wars, and a Korean War, took millions of young people to parts of the world they would never have been aware of. The A-bomb and the continuing Cold War shrank the globe until Main Streets all over the world seemed to be in our own backyards. Everyday life in America could never thereafter be the same —the everyday life of the *mind,* that is, however regular and stabilizing the day-to-day duties and pleasures might be.

Wherever you live today, if you ask your next-door neighbor how he thinks of himself in terms of class structures he will probably say he belongs to the middle classes. Few people, however limited their opportunities, would identify themselves as members of the "lower classes," and millionaires, nowadays, are more likely to try to hide the fact that they are wealthy than to engage in conspicuous display. This doesn't mean, of course, that there is not a class structure in American society, which sociologists try to identify as "upper-upper, lower-upper, upper-middle, lower-middle," etc. Such stratifications depend not so much on family background and lineage as upon occupational or educational status—and even more upon financial competence. Nevertheless the self-image of most Americans is essentially middle-class, and as technology has made available for more people what would have been luxuries in 1900, the lines of class distinction become dimmer. The truck driver has the same TV set as the banker; his family Chevrolet looks much like the banker's Cadillac; he sees the same movies (only more of them); he sleeps under the same kind of electric blanket; and even if he plays golf at the municipal course instead of the country club he has just as large a set of clubs.

Even in terms of financial status our society has moved toward greater uniformity. There are still great distinctions in wealth, but there are fewer of the very rich and fewer who are starving than there used to be. If you define the middle classes statistically as those families with incomes between $6,000 and $15,000, the percentage of such families grew from 13 percent in 1936 to 47 percent today. This does not mean that poverty is not at present a disturbing problem in the United States, the more so because it seems to be a hidden problem. It is true that if you define a poor family as one that has an income under $4,000, the percentage has dropped from 68 percent in 1935–36 to 23 percent in 1960 (all this in terms of the dollar value of 1960). But if you use the $4,000-per-family figure as a cutoff, recent studies have shown that 38 million people (over a fifth of the nation) are now living in poverty. Some 3.5 million Americans are in families with under $1,000-a-year income. The average per capita income of our "senior citizens"—those over sixty-five—is about $1,000 a year. This is real poverty, not much relieved by the fact that 23 percent of those earning less than $1,000 a year own cars.

In spite of these unhappy statistics, however, the "visibility" of the United States has been that of a middle-class structure. What kind of life have these people lived? More particularly, just now, what kind of homes have they inhabited and how have they decorated them? What kind of chairs have they sat on and what pictures have they hung on the walls? Here we get into areas of changing tastes, where one generation's art or hairdo becomes the laughingstock of the next.

If you had been dropped into the residential section of an American town in the early part of the century you would have found most houses neither notably beautiful nor abysmally ugly. Most of them were squarish brick or wood boxes, set in a sizable yard and shrouded gratefully by trees which softened their harsher contours. Typically they had big front porches where the family could sit in rocking chairs on a warm summer's evening and watch the horses and buggies, and an occasional Ford, go by. Each had its own back porch and a big attic and cellar. These houses had no pretension to architectural style; they sprang from a book of plans or a builder's brain. There were, to be sure, various layers of architectural or regional differences. Some houses would be clean Colonial or Cape Cod, others would be architectural monstrosities surviving from the period after the Civil War when "Carpenter's Gothic" was the rage—a confusion of pointed towers, useless turrets, and eccentric dormer windows, all ornamented by jigsaw scrollwork and grotesque decoration, a sort of nightmare architecture. Sometimes you would find a surviving "Queen Anne" house, a relic of what the builder thought was "quaint" or "picturesque" in the later nineteenth century, dressed up with "ornamental" chimneys and swallowed by a rash of cornices and bulging excrescences.

Other sections of town might represent a hodgepodge of builders' choices in the *beaux-arts* style popularized by the Chicago World Fair of 1893—a mixed grill of Greek, Roman, and Renaissance. Any kind of purity of style was overwhelmed by a random eclecticism ranging from "Egyptian" to "Byzantine" cottages to "Italian" villas. People were trying to be comfortable, or stylish, in the surroundings of a past that never really existed. There was, however, one kind of organic architecture that came in, as it were, by the back door. Infiltrating the Middle West and the East was an importation from California called the "bungalow," a wooden cottage marked by big overhanging eaves, cob-

57

Though built in the 1880's, the Carson Mansion at Eureka, California, is still a tourist attraction.

blestone chimneys, and big windows. Though it frequently became degraded in the builder's hands, it gave to the early century a new kind of freshness and honesty. As a matter of fact, though, the most eccentric creators of pseudo-Gothic or Queen Anne houses always prided themselves on the "sincerity" of their architecture—sincerity being a strangely ambiguous term.

But the average house made no pretense of style, and its plan fitted the way of life that went on within. A conventional arrangement was a front entrance into a large hall bedecked with a mirror, umbrella stand, and hat rack. On one side of this was the parlor, the least-used room in the house, shut up tight except on formal occasions and always smelling a little musty (there was a typical "parlor odor"). Here were the best chairs, ranging from heavy dark mahogany to fragile horsehair-covered antiques; a boldly flowered rug or carpet, and a marble-topped table displaying one or two of the best-looking books in the house: very probably Elbert Hubbard's *Message to Garcia* or *Little Journeys to the Homes of Great Men,* bound in limp leather. Perhaps, too, artificial flowers under a glass bell, and a stereoscopic viewer with scenes of Niagara Falls and Harper's Ferry. Children entered this room only on special occasions, and a little hushed.

On the other side of the hall was the living room or sitting room containing the comfortable chairs and the books that were to be read. Here in the first part of the century

An evening at home in the décor of 1907

"Mission" furniture of the early 1900's

was the mission furniture which laid such heavy loads on so many floors—massive oak tables and chairs, solid, uncompromisingly uncomfortable, but combining in their straight lines and unornamented contours a frank combination of simplicity and durability. Beyond this, through an arch hung with shell or bead portieres, was the dining room, with a big sideboard, and glass cupboards to protect the more fragile china. Here again the golden-oak table and chairs were solid and heavy. If the family had a "hired girl," meals were served here. More frequently they were eaten in the big kitchen beyond. Upstairs, of course, were the bedrooms (all houses had two stories), and if the house was big and grandmother was not living with the family (as she often was), a "spare room" as immaculate and chill as the parlor below. And above this the attic, a treasure-house of cast-off trunks and chests of drawers for children to explore on rainy days.

Within this little world the steady routines of family life flowed on. All rooms were wallpapered, of course, in whatever style happened to be current, and on the walls were hung the pictures which suited the family sense of beauty. Few of them were originals, for neither custom nor pocketbook dictated such expenditures. Frequently there were line engravings of some historical scene—"Washington Crossing the Delaware" was popular—or a sentimental family genre picture like "Breaking Home Ties." Rosa Bonheur's "The Horse Fair" and Landseer's pictures of noble dogs or stags-at-bay were great favorites. Color prints were likely to run to scenes of "The Burning of Rome" or G. A. Watts's

Luxury plumbing for families with maids, 1905

Left, "Goldilocks and the Three Bears," painted by Jesse Wilcox Smith. Above, a Harrison Fisher girl of 1907.

"Hope," displaying a strangely hopeless young woman sitting forlornly on a globe. Pictures that told stories were popular: Sandham's "The Village Smithy," or "Sleeping Innocence." Millet's landscape-religious picture "The Angelus" was found on many walls, as was Whistler's "Mother" (more accurately titled "Arrangement in Gray and Black, No. 1").

In the early nineteen-hundreds publishers were selling color prints, suitable for framing, by the well-known painters and illustrators of the time: Frederic Remington's "Western Types," watercolor drawings by Harrison Fisher, paintings of lovely women by Henry Hutt, pastels by Howard Chandler Christy, oils by Howard Pyle. For several decades Maxfield Parrish entered many American homes

Left, "Shedding Light" by Maxfield Parrish, 1918. Above, "Off
to School" by W. T. Smedley.
Below, "Attack on the Supply
Train" by Frederic Remington.

The residence of W. K. Vanderbilt in New York City

with his brilliantly violet and purple and rose pictures of romanticized castles in the clouds, or of decoratively sexless figures draped before backgrounds of never-never trees and mountains. His "Daybreak" sold a million copies in the late teens and early twenties. Occasionally a Corot or a Dutch genre print would appear, and even in good Protes-

"The Breakers" at Newport, Rhode Island

tant homes a Holy Family from the Italian Renaissance. But the general taste ran to "calendar" art in bold colors or to pictures which "said something" in terms of a narrative situation.

In the twenties domestic architecture became more frankly imitative and derivative than in the earlier years. The magnates of great wealth had for some time been adorning the eastern countryside with massive and magnificent structures which gave them a chance to display their fortunes in what Thorsten Veblen called "the barbarous warfare of competitive consumption." Lacking cultural roots or any elements of original good taste, they turned for their inspiration to Europe and its historic tradition of magnificence. William K. Vanderbilt had erected a huge French château on Fifth Avenue in 1881 at a cost of $3 million. Later George Vanderbilt constructed Biltmore, a lavish forest of roofs and chimneys based on the

An "English half-timber" house

Château de Blois. In 1914 Henry Clay Frick built on Fifth Avenue a mansion that cost $5.5 million. During these years, too, the rich were building at Newport, Rhode Island, elaborate and pretentious "cottages" which needed staffs of thirty servants and received, without bulging perceptibly, some 250 guests for Sunday lunch. Here were the Marble House, the Breakers, the Elms—the latter surrounded by landscaped terraces, ornamental walks, lawns and fountains, three bronze statues, and two teahouses. It was built at the turn of the century, when Andrew Carnegie's personal income, for example, was more than $23 million a year and there was no income tax to pay.

The decline and ultimate destruction or decay of these ostentatious structures, whether in New York or Newport, underlines a whole sequence of social and economic history

66

The Robie House designed by Frank Lloyd Wright

in the United States. They are ghosts of a vanished civilization. The new income taxes bit deeply into such expansive living, nor could servants be found to run the huge mausoleums. Somehow, too, the marble palaces seemed a little out of place during the depression years of the nineteen-thirties. Many of them have since been leveled to save taxes. Some of the Newport "cottages" now receive gaping tourists at $1.75 a head; others have been turned into girls' schools or apartments. It was reported that in the 1960's, in The Waves, built in 1927, a four-bedroom, two-bath apartment was fitted into what was once the dining room.

All this was a part of America, though it would be inaccurate to say that it represented "everyday life" for very many people—except in the Sunday supplements!

But in the boom days of the twenties many citizens of more modest means built houses which were simply cut-down versions of those Venetian palaces, French châteaux, or stately homes. The Elizabethan Picturesque laid a heavy hand on architects. These were merely "adaptations" of imitations of traditions which, it was felt, must be distinguished because they were European. The decade saw the proliferation of Dutch Colonial, Italian Derivative, Italian Renaissance, West Coast Spanish, Florida Spanish, Norman Manor, Tudor Half-Timber, and so on. People seemed not to feel the need of an organic architecture adapted to the needs of the region and time, an architecture which would make sense in human terms in its own day, thus creating its own style.

Even before World War II, however, there were stirrings toward something new—new in the sense of an architecture which was not so much picturesque as suitable to the needs of modern living. Some years before, Henry H. Richardson and Louis Sullivan, of the so-called "Chicago school," had been pointing the way to the use of indigenous materials and to designs which had a new kind of rambling freedom and their own comfortable beauty. Even in the imitative

A Gropius modern of 1938

"Modern" architecture of 1936

period of the twenties one of the later giants of American architecture was well on his way toward the creation of an "organic" architecture, which meant, as he said, that "form derives its structure from nature and from the character of the material and its conditions, exactly as a flower forms itself according to the law which lies in the seed." Frank Lloyd Wright believed that homes should have a sense of *shelter,* that architecture should be based on the idea of enclosed space rather than mass, and that spaces should flow into one another rhythmically.

The American public was slow to accept Wright's ideas, however, and the late twenties and the thirties saw a growing interest in a European version of modern architecture which came to be known as the "international style." The names here were Gropius, Mies van der Rohe, Neutra, Le Corbusier. Corbusier said that a home should be "a machine for living," and the impact of the machine age was strong upon this style. It emphasized rectilinear shapes, geometric

Neutra modern of 1938

regularity, a cool and functional simplicity sometimes verging on the monotonous. It had the virtues of absence of sham and clutter and an emphasis upon the relationship between indoors and outdoors. Yet as it was practiced at first in the United States it seemed sterile and not always even functional. The furniture which was designed to fill these houses was eccentric, too: chairs and tables of bent chrome-steel tubing, angular and uncomfortable; bookcases stepped up like skyscrapers. Flat roofs, walls of windows allowing for little privacy—these came to be associated with what was called in the thirties "modernistic" architecture. Most folk didn't like it much; these excrescences looked strange on streets given over to Dutch Colonial and Miami Spanish.

But the big architectural change was rolling, typified, in its styles and their acceptance, by the changes in the words used to describe it—from "modernistic," with its contemptuous overtones, to "modern," a neutral attitude, to "contemporary," a recognition of acceptance. What would become known as the American "vernacular" was marked by purity of style, simplicity of structural arrangement, and ease of construction. It retained the textured surfaces and the airiness of the international style but refined its angularities and warmed its chilly (aseptic) feeling. It emerged at its most typical in variations of the so-called "ranch house" style developed first in California, marked by flat or low-pitched roofs, wide eaves, and an orientation toward the back with its patio or outdoor living space. The front porch disappeared, for nobody sat on front porches any more. Always there was the big picture window, which was fine as long as there was an outdoor picture for it to frame. But as this style, or its modifications, became the accepted dialect of contemporary architecture and determined the style of housing developments all over the country, frequently the obligatory picture window framed only its owner's garbage pail or the picture window next door. Nevertheless the new houses have become an accepted part of the American scene, functional without being self-consciously so, flexible and informal, and capable of a wide variety of adaptations.

The interiors of these houses are also a record of chang-

California ranch house of 1938

ing American tastes. They are adaptable to almost any kind of furnishings, including replicas of early American chairs and stools and shoemakers' benches which still furnish a good deal of work for Grand Rapids. More typically, however, the furniture is casual and comfortable, with clean straight lines. Cupboards, couches, chests of drawers, and bookcases are often built in as part of the architecture. The structural materials themselves (brick, cement block, the very beams of the roof) can become the textured décor of the interior.

As for pictures—there is often little wall space for them. When they do appear (and by no means all of the nation lives in "contemporary" houses) they usually do not resemble those of the early part of the century, any more than the hi-fi set plays "Silver Threads Among the Gold." What kinds of pictures do hang on our walls?

Many people still like artistic realism in their landscapes and flower pictures. One of the best sellers among color prints today is "Fiery Peaks," a golden-orange picture of the Cascade Mountains at sunset. Nevertheless on many walls hang pictures which would have been inconceivable there half a century ago. I don't mean Rembrandt's "Aristotle Contemplating the Bust of Homer," though thousands of prints of that picture have been sold since its purchase by the Metropolitan Museum for $2.3 million (one suspects that dollar value and popularity have some connection here). No, to trace the major shift—a delayed one, to be sure—in American artistic taste one needs to go back to 1913, and the famous Armory Show in New York.

This first full-flung display of modern art in the United States proved to be not so much an exhibition as an earthquake. For the first time the public, as well as museums and art collectors, was confronted with an art they had succeeded in ignoring up to then. Here were paintings by

The "Armory Show" of 1913

Matisse, Picasso, Degas, Seurat, Léger, Derain, Gauguin—seemingly grotesque distortions which puzzled, bewildered, angered, but somehow fascinated the people who flocked to see them. Most of the critics took cubism and Postimpressionism as a personal insult to their dignity. One of them called Gauguin "a decorator tainted with insanity"; another described Marcel Duchamp's cubistic "Nude Descending a Staircase" as "an explosion in a shingle factory." Among the milder phrases used were "the chatter of anarchistic monkeys"; "the total destruction of the art of painting"; "the licentiousness of over-estheticism, the madness of ultra culture"; "paranoiacs"; "madhouse design," "unbalanced fanatics."

The strange thing was that first museums and then collectors began to buy these so-called monstrosities. The Americans in the show—John Marin, Stuart Davis, Edward Hopper, Walt Kuhn—who had been ignored where they had not been despised, went on to become American classics. French impressionism and postimpressionism be-

73

Duchamp's "Nude Descending a Staircase"

came a staple of the art galleries. At first displayed only in the homes of the avant-garde, this art survived the cultural lag which always inhibits the acceptance of such movements. During the twenties and thirties it was at best tolerated by the public; in the fifties it was loved. By the sixties good color prints of this "insane" art were decorating many American homes, about the time that it was beginning to be considered outdated by those to whom the nonrepresentational forms of abstract expressionism—creations in pure form, color, and design—were the wave of the future. Today the reception rooms of many American businesses (not usually the pioneer fringe of art appreciation) are hung with Picassos and Marins and Gauguins. Printmakers say that almost any painting by Utrillo will rack up record sales. Van Gogh is a perennial favorite. Picasso's "Woman in White" has sold nearly a million copies. The vastly improved quality and the cheapness of color prints in recent years have undoubtedly done much to stimulate sales. In 1950, only 326 such prints were copyrighted; in 1961, 3,255. Many people can buy them at their supermarkets.

More recent modern art is still controversial, and it is difficult to see how the reaction against academic naturalism can go further than abstract expressionism. Like other arts of post-World War II, it is frequently violent, obviously in revolt, often devoted to an assault upon the senses. If it is the modern image of man, it is thought by some critics to be an image vicious, decayed, tortured, filled with agony and death. It may be that such expressions of frustration will reach their own dead end—or their own purification; but in the meantime, such is the history of American taste and its delayed acceptances, that it would be foolish to say that some of the best of this art, too, might not be found one day on the walls of many American homes. It is, at least, a view of modern life which is of a piece with the plays of Edward Albee and Jean Genêt, and the novels of James Jones and Norman Mailer.

Any discussion of the life of Americans in terms of the towns they have built, the homes they have lived in, and the way they have decorated those homes would be incomplete without looking at a shift in population patterns which has helped to determine the way of life of millions of people. This might be called the Flight to the Suburbs, or the Day of the Tract Developer.

Each city has always had its suburbs, but in the earlier years of the century they consisted of belts of residential districts still closely attached to the central complex, and never more than a short streetcar ride away from office or

Levittown, Pennsylvania, typical of housing developments of the 1950's

factory. As cities grew and their more nearly central residential portions decayed, the big houses that lined Euclid or Fifth Avenue were deserted by their owners, who moved to districts farther out. The process was a slow one, however, and the city still operated as an integral unit, dominating its peripheral groups of houses. To be sure, there were always commuters to New York City from Greenwich, Connecticut, or Princeton, New Jersey, but they were a small part of the whole. After 1945, however, a new phenomenon swept the country. The cities themselves stopped growing, even though more and more people were being drawn into outlying metropolitan areas. The metropolis itself was exploding outward into a network of related collateral towns. Small rural villages on the new superhighways leading into the city suddenly found themselves suffering all the delights—and the growing pains—of larger towns. Young couples, understandably, no longer wanted to raise their families in apartments on crowded city streets. So they decided to combine the necessity of earning a living in the city with the pleasures of living in the countryside, or something approximating the countryside—at least out where trees grew and there were lawns to mow.

So when the existing suburbs could no longer contain the influx, we entered the period of the bulldozer, and the methodical chopping up of the landscape into a network of entirely new communities accessible to the cities or to the new industries which had decentralized themselves. "Dormitory" suburbs, they were called, where the husband fought congested traffic each morning, and then the same traffic in the evening to get home in time for a late dinner and if possible to see his children to bed. Only on weekends could he tire his muscles in gardening or mowing; and since he really *did* tire, the power mower soon became a sign of status.

The automobile made all this possible. The result was hundreds of large mass-fabricated communities, neither truly rural nor truly urban, planted on the countryside with all their streets and schools and churches and shopping centers. Ambitious builders were unconcerned about the prospective slums they were sometimes creating—the networks of telephone-and-power poles dominating a monotonous series of duplicate houses which became a rash on the landscape. But they were "homes in the country" for the civically disinherited who were happy to trade the horrors of city life for the gentler horrors of the new suburbia. Between 1950 and 1960 many cities actually lost population while the metropolitan suburbs were growing with the rapidity of a stampede. Across the nation, suburban areas increased six times faster in population growth than cities, and accounted for nearly two-thirds of the 24 million population growth from 1950 to 1959.

It was a way of life which people happily accepted; it was not forced on them. Though sleazy community planning and building, with minimal standards of order and beauty, brought its disappointments, suburbanism was here to stay. To say that its inhabitants are unhappy with their barbecue pits and their neighborhood parties is to adopt the worries of the sociologists who have found that decentralization—or a combination of new centralizations—does not insure Utopia. The father suffers and the mother is bound to the wheel of child rearing and child transportation and housekeeping; but the children seem to thrive. The sociologists worry, too, with some point, about the depressing effect of the uniformities of such a civilization: its pressures toward conformity with the closely herded community group, its emphasis on group structure both in child rearing and industrial organization. But if, as has been claimed, we are shifting our national character in the direction of a loss of individuality and a colorless conformity with our immediate social environment, it would be unfair to lay all this on the lap of suburbia. No one has proved that for the purposes of healthy family life it is worse than the downtown row of solid brick apartments which would be one of its alternatives.

3

The People Read:
Books and Magazines

To explore any facet of American life since 1900 is always to be reminded how that life has changed, not only in terms of its physical environment but also in its human attitudes and ideals and standards. So much that was taken for granted in 1900 seems laughable or merely quaint now; so much that is taken for granted now would have seemed outrageously bizarre or shocking to our grandfathers at the turn of the century.

One change is clear: progressively more Americans have been buying more books and magazines. In 1904 newspapers and periodicals had a total circulation of about 50 million; in 1960 of about 400 million, while the population was just a little more than doubling. Thus too in the publishing of books. In 1900, 4,490 new books were published, including pamphlets; in 1963, 19,057 new hard-cover books, *not* including pamphlets. And in 1958 over 97 million hardbound "general" books for adults were sold—not including technical books, textbooks, or Bibles. Two-thirds of these were distributed by book clubs. In 1960, 85 different book clubs sold 80 million copies of books. Literacy, if not necessarily good taste, has mushroomed.

Books popular in 1908 included *Beverly of Graustark, To Have and To Hold, The Little Shepherd of Kingdom Come, The Call of the Wild, The Virginian,* and *The Crisis.*

Since the life of the mind is not the least important index of American civilization, it is important to see just what people were reading.

Fiction was outselling nonfiction in 1900 by more than two to one, and would continue to outsell it for a quarter of a century. There were definite tastes indicated by this fiction. Not many people were reading the new "harsh" realists: Thomas Hardy, Frank Norris, Theodore Dreiser. General Lew Wallace's *Ben Hur,* first published in 1880, was known to everyone and was still selling widely. Another novel about the early Christians, Henry Sienkiewicz's *Quo Vadis,* competed with *Ben Hur* in popularity. Both would appear in many dramatizations and in at least one movie spectacular each succeeding generation. Much new fiction was either romantic or historical, usually both. Sentimental cloak-and-sword novels, frequently set in mythical kingdoms, flooded the presses—books like *The Prisoner of Zenda, Graustark, When Knighthood Was in Flower, To Have and to Hold, In the Palace of the King.* There were regional novels: stories about the Old West just about the time the Old West was disappearing (Owen Wister's *The Virginian,* in 1902, was the first and one of the best of these); stories about the Old South and the happy good-Negroes on the plantations (Thomas Dixon's *The Clansman* was said to have sold 40,000 copies during ten days in

1905). John Fox's *The Little Shepherd of Kingdom Come* (1903) was set in the Cumberland Mountains and his *The Trail of the Lonesome Pine* (1908) in Kentucky.

All these best-selling novels had certain qualities in common. They were in what was known as the "genteel tradition"; their heroes were clean fresh young Americans, pure in heart even when cowboys. Their view of life was cheery and optimistic. True love and noble simplicity, though sometimes in difficulty, were always triumphant in the end. Such a novel, for example, as Westcott's *David Harum,* which by 1901 had sold over 400,000 copies and finally reached a total of 1.2 million, was nostalgically and warmly simple, as well as being a tribute to crusty Yankee shrewdness. None of these novels reflected life with any depth or accuracy, and they were immensely popular in an age of innocence.

Following these, in the period up through World War I, came a run of novels pretty much alike in tone, whether written by Alice Hegan Rice, Kate Douglas Wiggin, Gene Stratton Porter, or Eleanor H. Porter. They were novels of the "happiness" school of writing, soggy with benevolence and pathos, telling stories in which the characters, like the readers, could smile through their tears and revel in a mawkish optimism. Thus *Mrs. Wiggs of the Cabbage Patch, Rebecca of Sunnybrook Farm, A Girl of the Limberlost,* which sold 2 million copies from 1910 on, and *Laddie,* which sold 1.5 million. Eleanor Porter's *Pollyanna* in 1913, the story of the "glad girl," reached the depths, or height, of this sort of thing. It got a word into the dictionary (not an easy thing to do): "Pollyanna: a blindly optimistic girl."

Equally unreal, though a good deal more exciting, were the Westerns which gained their great momentum about this time with the novels of Zane Grey and set the pattern which was to become the bread-and-butter of the movies

81

and finally of television. Their heroes were strong and simple, the stories black-and-white narratives about cowboys and cattle rustlers and horse thieves and noble sheriffs. Zane Grey was on nine best-seller lists between 1915 and 1934, and by 1945 (the taste lingered on!) his 63 novels had sold over 19 million copies. Their only rival was Edgar Rice Burroughs with his *Tarzan of the Apes* and its 30 sequels, which sold 25 million copies.

Tarzan was popular with both young and old, but many of the most successful books were written especially for the "American youth." British author G. A. Henty's exciting historical novels had been standard fare before 1900. He wrote some 80 stories of adventure, with such titles as *Under Drake's Flag, Among the Malay Pirates, With Clive in India,* and *True to the Old Flag.* No writer did more, however, both to entertain and to solidify what has since come to be called the "Protestant Ethic," than Horatio Alger, Jr. He wrote 135 novels (or one novel 135 times) and their sales have been estimated variously from 17 to 200 million copies. They preached the virtues of thrift, frugality, punctuality, industriousness, sobriety, and obedience, but "luck" was often a major element. *The Youth's Companion,* advertising Alger's novels in 1909, stated his themes succinctly: "The author invariably selects as the basis for his writings a boy whose beginning is humble and unpromising, and graphically describes his rise to wealth and fame." Virtue always led to success and to the poor boy's triumph over the town bully or the selfish banker. Thus *Do and Dare; Hector's Inheritance; The Erie Train Boy; Tom, the Bootblack; Paul, the Peddler;* and *Struggling Upward.* This last title epitomizes the "American success" dream which was deeply rooted in our society.

Still more thrilling tales awaited the young reader, as in the immensely popular Frank Merriwell stories. Frank lived

One of Horatio Alger's novels

dangerously, but his character was so solid and true that (with a little luck) he always won out over his adversaries. There were some 200 volumes in the series. Frank's creator, "Burt L. Standish" (William G. Patten) sent Frank into the jungle, up mountains, into mines. He went first to Fardale School, where he was the sworn enemy of school bullies, and later to Yale, from which he was finally graduated after a series of adventures which would have shattered most students. One gathers that Yale would never have triumphed over Harvard in football but for Frank Merriwell.

A Frank Merriwell story featured in a youth magazine

He was the American Boy, the forerunner of the heroes of other juvenile series such as *The Rover Boys* (5 million copies sold), the *Motor Boat Boys,* the *Tom Swift* books. Most youngsters today, fed on comic books and science fiction, would find these unsophisticated stories naïve and flat. But they are remembered tenderly by many people now alive, some of whom may still believe that there must have been a real Merriwell at Yale.

Poetry was not much read in the first quarter of the century—nor is it now—but a few versifiers had astounding success. Thus Robert W. Service, whose *Songs of a Sour-*

dough and *Ballads of a Cheechako* did for the gold country of Alaska what Zane Grey did for Wyoming. Even if they didn't recite it on occasion, there were few young men who didn't know by heart "The Shooting of Dan McGrew." Still more popular and folksy and sentimental were the soporific banalities of Edgar ("Eddie") Guest. He was in the tradition of James Whitcomb Riley, the Hoosier poet, who also dealt in humor and pathos, as in his book of verse *When the Frost Is on the Punkin* (1911). But Riley had a homely honesty, particularly in his poems about childhood, which ultimately won him the gold medal of the National Institute of Arts and Letters. Guest followed Riley, but from afar. He manufactured by the mile his homespun colloquialisms and his limp celebrations of God, babies, pie, and porch-sitting.

> Ain't it good when life seems dreary
> And your hopes about to end,
> Just to feel the handclasp cheery
> Of a fine old loyal friend?

He was writing for what he called "jes' plain folks," and there must have been a good many of them who liked his brand of corn, for his volume *A Heap o' Livin'* went through 35 printings and sold more than a million copies. He was syndicated, at one time, in 275 newspapers. If we are looking for everyday life in the first quarter of the century, Guest must have been a significant part of it. As one thinks back, it is strange that "home" and "mother," two reasonably significant components of life, should have their greatest popular recognition in shoddy doggerel.

It is true that watery sentiment and stereotyped romance was no special possession of the early twentieth century; cheap fiction, representing views of life just as hollow if a good deal different, is widely popular today. But in the years

85

The cover for *Main Street*, by Sinclair Lewis, 1920

after World War I a new kind of assessment of modern life began to revolutionize the novel. During the twenties Sinclair Lewis made the best-seller lists with *Main Street* and *Babbitt* (another word in the dictionary), clinical dissections of small-town America. John Dos Passos, in *Manhattan Transfer* and *U.S.A.*, drew kaleidoscopic pictures of a chaotic American life far removed from dreamy escape literature. Ernest Hemingway, although somewhat sentimentally attached to violence, wrote exactly and simply, glorifying courage and endurance. With the thirties, and the Great Depression, John Steinbeck shocked his fellow countrymen into a kind of compassion, or at least a recognition, concerning the horrors of life among the migrant workers in California. And the greatest of all of them, William Faulkner, was creating his intimate geography of Yoknapatawpha County and its morbidly repellent if uncompromisingly real inhabitants. (Faulkner did not make the best-seller lists, however, until the paperbacks came along, and then it was with what he called his "potboiler," *Sanctuary*.) A new kind of realism had infiltrated the American novel, and after World War II the everyday American was subjected to even stronger doses of grimness.

Unlike the days of 1917, when America went into a World War flying the flags and singing the songs of a romantic idealism, World War II was fought in full recognition of its bitterness; and its aftertaste, in the fiction which described it, was bitter too. With the multiple confusions of the fifties and the sixties fiction became savagely disillusioned about life. There were no more heroes—not even non-heroes—but rather anti-heroes, angry young men who

Sinclair Lewis driving a 1915 Ford

found little but despair and violence and unhappy sex and degeneracy and moral chaos in the world around them. They found no place for affirmation in life, and in many instances the authors in their novels conducted their psychoanalysis in public, so to speak, in the guise of the self-destructive neuroticisms of their leading characters. One need not believe in Eddie Guest to assume that while the disappearance of the sentimental hero may be a salutary thing, areas of dignity and belief may still exist in life. One hopes that more writers will turn away from the wailing wall to discover an affirmation, rather than a denial of the potentially good in human nature. It is true that great writers through the ages, from Sophocles to Shakespeare, have not dealt with the normal life of average man—most men do not marry their mothers or murder their uncles. But great writers have never pretended that the exceptional was the universal, nor did they ever deny the essential worthiness of men. Most people are perplexed and confused today (the Eden of 1900 seems far away), but they have not, I think, given up, to immerse themselves in despair.

It is worth noting how, in times of stress, people have always turned to "peace of mind" books. In the early century such books were frankly religious. Later on, the religion got watered down to a kind of ethical benevolence, or was shown to have immediate practical values in the world of affairs, as in Henry C. Link's *The Return to Religion*. Joshua Liebman's *Peace of Mind* was on the nonfiction best-seller lists for two consecutive years, 1947–48. Fulton J. Sheen's *Life Is Worth Living* and *Peace of Soul* sold a quarter of a million each. As far back as 1922 Émile Coué found the recipe for success (and big sales) in *Self-Mastery Through Conscious Autosuggestion*. All you needed to do was to keep telling yourself: "Every day in every way I am getting better and better." Americans have always hunted for short-cuts to satisfaction.

Modern critics keep questioning the importance that religion has in everyday life for most people. If books on religious topics are any indication, however, we have always been concerned about food for the soul. The all-time sales record in the twentieth century *for any book of any kind* (excepting always the Bible) is for one by a Congregational minister, Charles M. Sheldon. His novel *In His Steps* (1897) was an attempt to show what would happen if everyone based his actions on the question: "What would Jesus do?" His answers seem a little dated now, but the book sold an estimated 8 million copies; you can still buy it in paperback. Among the other books which have sold 3 million or more copies in our century are Jesse Hurlbut's *Story of the Bible* (1904) and Fulton Oursler's *The Greatest Story Ever Told* (1949). In the 1940's during World War II people were reading such books as *The Robe, The Keys of the Kingdom,* and *The Big Fisherman.*

The Bible itself, of course, remains always the runaway best seller. In 1958, 19 million Bibles and Testaments were sold in the United States. This was over twice as many as the 9 million sold in 1947, and the comparison of figures would not indicate much decline in religious interest.

The supposition that Americans have always been a practical and pragmatic people is confirmed by the steady popularity of how-to-do-it books—a type of publication which has recently been called "the non-book." Do you want to fix the plumbing or build a summer home or improve your mind or win at bridge or become a TV actor or raise children or be socially correct or win friends? There are many books to tell you how to do each of these. Dale Carnegie's *How to Win Friends and Influence People*

(1936) sold nearly 5 million copies. On the best-seller list for 1950 was *How I Raised Myself from Failure to Success in Selling,* and on the lists for both 1959 and 1960 was *How I Turned $1,000 into a Million in Real Estate.* (Barnum was an American.) People in the 1900's were no less eager for self-instruction: in 1903, Doubleday, Page and Co. advertised *How to Make Rugs, How to Study Shakespeare, How to Make Money,* and *How to Keep Well.*

This last area of self-help has led millions of Americans who retain, perhaps, some primitive suspicion of professional medicine, to buy a whole spate of health books which recommend a return to nature's ways of living and eating, plus diet books which teach you, presumably, how to lose that gross fat without cutting out any food you really like. One of the great best sellers of 1959 and 1960 was D. C. Jarvis's *Folk Medicine.* This had the beautiful simplicity of advocating doses of honey and vinegar to cure illnesses. A decade earlier the fad was Gaylord Hauser's blackstrap molasses; a quarter of a million people bought his *Look Younger, Live Longer.* Here was the perfect title, emphasizing as it did the American's hunger for eternal youth and the desire of most people to outlive their neighbors.

Of all the how-to-do-it books, cookbooks have over the years had the most gigantic sales. On the all-time best-seller list since the turn of the century, five of the 23 books which sold over 3 million copies apiece were cookbooks. In the first six months of 1963, 40 new cookbooks were published in the United States. Here, in the literal sense, one can trace changes in taste! In the early century most people favored good plain American cooking, and make no mistake about it!—meat and potatoes and pie. Recipes were collected and published, many of them in local editions, by women who might be a little vague about the exact measurements, for many of them cooked by instinct: "a pinch of this"; "season to taste." But they knew what their generation liked. A little later America discovered France, and Escoffier and his more simplified adaptations came into the home as "the art of French cooking." Cooking with herbs became popular and today many kitchens are lined with rows of herbs which grandmother never heard of. More recently, when the man of the house began to don an apron and cap suitable for the "cookout," barbecue cookbooks became popular. Today there are blender cookbooks and mixer cookbooks. In recent years we have had a resurgence of the coyness which often afflicts writers of cookbooks, so that recipes become not so much directions as to what to do as cute comments on how to eat in bed or how to cook if you hate cooking. But no matter what the approach might be, few publishers have lost money on cookbooks.

Cookbooks, by definition, should be nonfiction. It is a comment on the changing interests of Americans that whereas fiction outsold nonfiction two to one in 1900, the preponderance is now in the opposite direction; nonfiction today outsells fiction many times over. There are several reasons for this reversal aside from what critics call the low state of novel writing today. People are much more concerned than they used to be with the world around them—political, scientific, historical, economic, sociological. They live in that world much more intimately than they did in 1900, and they are eager to understand it and find meanings in it. One is always slightly startled to discover that the world of science has the habit of catching up with science fiction!

The greatest development in the world of publishing has been the astounding success of the paperback book. We did not invent it—Europe had had it for many years—but since 1939, when it got its start here, it has become one of the

THE SPRING FASHION NUMBER
THE LADIES' HOME JOURNAL

MARCH 1907   THE CURTIS PUBLISHING COMPANY, PHILADELPHIA   FIFTEEN CENTS

Cover of a famous magazine for ladies, 1907

most exciting cultural developments of our time. No one can avoid being touched by it. Some 24,000 titles were in print in 1964, and this was an increase of almost one-third over the previous year. About 310 million copies were sold in 1962. Of these, nearly 37 million were religious books of one kind or another and 108 million were textbooks or workbooks. Nevertheless a significant proportion, some 76 million, were what are known as "quality" books.

The whole thing was a revolution in merchandising as well as in printing. No longer does one have to hunt up one of the 1,700 bookstores in the country to find a good book; it can be picked up in the nearest drugstore, supermarket, newsstand, or bus station. The cheapness and convenience of the paperback and the fact that many hundreds of significant works are published in this form each year does not of course mean that the American public has become uniformly highbrow. The titles, and even more the covers, are evidence that trash abounds. Nor are the best sellers usually the books of distinction. *Peyton Place* and *God's Little Acre* sold their 8 or 9 million copies apiece. Of the 20 best-selling paperbacks since 1939 half have been by Mickey Spillane and Erskine Caldwell—adventures in brutality and sex. But if you want to buy a good book today, from Sophocles to Freud to Matthew Arnold, you can get one cheap. William L. Shirer's *The Rise and Fall of the Third Reich* sold, in addition to its hard-cover bookstore sales and its book-club distribution, nearly 2 million copies in paperback. You can't laugh off the fact that somebody buys 1.2 million copies of Shakespeare every year, that Plato rubs shoulders with Dr. Spock, that Homer is right up there beside Hemingway.

Perhaps magazines, even more than books, reflect the interests of any given age. This is particularly true of their advertisements, of which we shall see more later. But the articles and stories that magazines print, their attitudes and crusades and their illustrations, give a vivid cross section of American taste. Or rather of many tastes (or lack of taste), for the multiplicities of appeal have always been stupendous.

To begin with, the sheer mass of periodical publication is impressive. If you count specialized "trade" magazines aimed at special audiences, the number today runs about 7,500. Even in 1900 there were over 6,000, covering all

M^cCLURE'S MAGAZINE

JOHN D ROCKEFELLER
A CHARACTER SKETCH BY IDA M. TARBELL

McClure's magazine, 1905

conceivable fields of politics, sports, science, religion, drama, music, art, fashion, fiction, humor, house-and-home. Today there are some 50 magazines with circulations of one million or over—11 with 5 million or over. Of the latter, six are aimed at women readers. Away out in front is the *Reader's Digest,* which in 1963 printed over 14 million copies of each issue. Any reader can find any kind of magazine he wants—and if he can't read, there are always the picture magazines!

Magazines have always been very sensitive barometers of entertainment or uplift, and the contrasts between 1900

The Youth's Companion in 1901

and today are highly informative. *The Youth's Companion,*
which sold over half a million copies a week in the early
part of the century and listed among its authors Theodore
Roosevelt, Jack London, O. Henry, Robert Frost and even
Winston Churchill, M.P., wouldn't sell a hundred copies
today. Its declared concern was for the welfare of youth.
"Let their minds be formed," it said, "their hearts prepared,
and their characters be moulded for the scenes and duties
of a brighter day." It languished in the period following
World War I and expired in 1927, about the same time
that two other important magazines for young people died:

Scribner's in 1901

The American Boy and *St. Nicholas*. At this distance they seem pretty dull and excessively moral. But *Playboy,* on the other hand, would have been inconceivable in 1900, a time when the relatively sedate *Police Gazette* was daring barber-shop reading.

The history of a magazine often reminds one of looking at an amoeba under a microscope: it grows, subdivides, dwindles, coalesces, is absorbed; it suffers change or dies. Here are the names of some magazines of 1900 which have disappeared: the humorous magazines, *Puck, Judge,* and

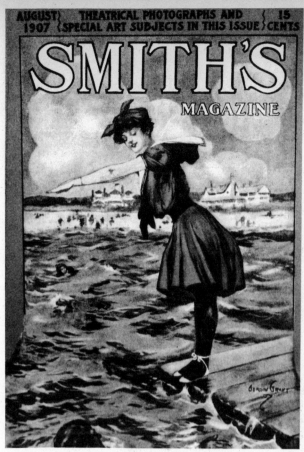

Smith's magazine in 1907

the old *Life; The Literary Digest, Scribner's, Century, The Living Age, The Forum, McClure's, Everybody's, Munsey's, Bluebook*. All these were gone by 1940. Of the 20 general magazines which had circulations of at least a million in 1926, nine vanished in the next 15 years. Those which have continued have succeeded in doing so by reflecting the changing times.

What were magazines like in the early nineteen-hundreds? First, the so-called "quality" publications such as *Harper's, The Atlantic Monthly, Scribner's, Century*. They never had

Cosmopolitan in 1908

mass circulations but they were impeccably decorous and correct. Readers were presented with articles on "The Colorado Sheep Ranch," "The Rise of the Country Club," "A Trip up the Rhine," "The Principal Foreign Buildings in Tientsin," "Daniel Webster," "Significant Knowledge of the Bible," "Expansion Through Reciprocity," and "Is Sentiment Declining?" (Yes: "The reign of science and reason has begun.") Stories were written by esteemed female authors with triple-plated names: Grace Ellery Channing, Caroline Brett McLean, Elizabeth Stuart Phelps, Josephine Daskin Brown. One writer in the *Atlantic*, which was still

Life (predecessor of today's *Life*), 1915

uncompromisingly Bostonian, traced the decline of "the New England woman," who was "too set on lofty duties to allow much of the *coquetterie,* or flirting, or a femininely accented *camaraderie* with men, such as the more elemental women of Chicago, Cincinnati, San Francisco, and New York enjoy." Here were the outposts of the respectable and the genteel—magazines which were filled, interestingly enough, with technically excellent color pictures by the famous illustrators of the day: Howard Pyle, Frederic Remington, James Montgomery Flagg, and Charles Dana Gibson. Young men languished after the clean-cut beauty of the "Gibson Girl"—who doesn't look so bad today, incidentally.

The early century saw the rise, too, of the new phenomenon, the mass-circulation magazine. New readers were being drawn literally by the millions to magazines selling for 10 or 15 cents, a price made possible by the discovery that, if you have enough advertising, you can almost afford to give your magazine away. One issue of the *Saturday Evening Post*, in 1929, ran to 272 pages, weighed two pounds, had reading matter for 20 hours and 20 minutes, and cost five cents. There were in that one issue 214 national advertisers, whose ads brought the Curtis Publishing Co. $1,512,000.

By 1900 the *Ladies' Home Journal* was selling a million copies a month at 10 cents each. Its famous editor, Edward Bok, was bullying the women of America into good taste in

Three studies of the "Gibson Girl" of Charles Dana Gibson

THE ETERNAL QUESTION

THE SATURDAY EVENING POST

Illustrated Weekly
A° D! Benj. Franklin

JULY 19, 1924   5 cts.

Ben Ames Williams—Harry Leon Wilson—James Hopper—Elizabeth Frazer
Garet Garrett—Ellis Parker Butler—Dana Burnet—Frederic F. Van de Water

The *Saturday Evening Post* in 1924

dress, household decoration, and architecture. He ran a series of plans for cheap, well-designed houses, one of which was by a young architect named Frank Lloyd Wright. Bok called bric-a-brac "the curse of the American home." The average woman, he wrote, "is a perfect slave to the useless rubbish in her rooms, which only offends the eye and accumulates dust." Along with its exhortations to women the *Journal* also gave advice to insure good health: "The head of the bed should, when convenient, be placed toward the north, especially for persons suffering from nervousness."

A James Montgomery Flagg illustration for *McClure's* in 1914. "What a bully thing life is!" he said, contemplating the moon with the air of an expert.

And it recorded that when the first mounted policeman appeared in New York City in November, 1914, he arrested a woman for smoking a cigarette on Fifth Avenue, even though she was in a car. Fashion note, also for 1914: "For gymnasium work, the school-girl wears a loose blouse and full bloomers coming to just beneath the knee, with black stockings." Note on labor and wages: in March, 1906, most housemaids rose at 4:30 A.M., and earned $10 a month. The good old days?

The period before World War I was also the heyday of such magazines as *Munsey's, McClure's,* and *Everybody's*—appealing to a whole new class of readers. Their fiction was rapid and forceful, their articles aimed at the everyday interests of the average middle-class citizen. These journals developed the "muckraking" school of writers, and such journalists as Lincoln Steffens, Ida M. Tarbell, Ray Stannard Baker, and David Graham Phillips attacked the monopolistic excesses of big business, and political corruption and graft in high places, from "The Shame of Minneapolis" to "The Treason of the Senate." Ida Tarbell wrote the history of the Standard Oil Co. for *McClure's,* and no one was more surprised than she when it turned into an account of rapacity and corruption. All this seemed like sensationalism, but the brutal facts spoke for themselves, even in the face of possible libel suits. Who today would attack a public figure as did Miss Tarbell in her 1905 article for *McClure's* entitled "John D. Rockefeller: A Character Study"? She concluded that the only explanation for the predatory career of the creator of the Standard Oil Company was that he was the victim of a money passion which blinded his sense of justice, his humanity, his affections; that he was literally money-mad. It is a comment on the American willingness to forget that years later the image of Mr. Rockefeller in the public mind was that of a benevolent old man giving away dimes to Florida children while he delivered little lectures on thrift. In the meantime, of course, he had established the major philanthropies of the Rockefeller Medical Institute and the Rockefeller Foundation. His grandson was to become governor of New York. All was forgiven.

By the twenties the climate of opinion had so changed that the big-circulation magazines like the *Saturday Evening Post* and particularly the *American Magazine* spent many of their pages glorifying the American businessman —his independence, his enterprise, his success.

To be sure, not all people in the early century were reading the *Atlantic* or *McClure's*. The old-fashioned "pulp" magazine, of which the publishing house of Street and Smith had the largest stable, was appealing to a different public. The familiar dime novel evolved into such magazines as *Buffalo Bill Stories, Jesse James Stories,* the *Nick Carter Weekly*—one of the first detective-story magazines. Here were tales of action and suspense and melodramatic escapes, but in contrast to such characters of the later mid-century as Mike Hammer and James Bond, Nick Carter did not drink, smoke, swear, or lie. He respected all women. Frederick Dey, the creator of Nick Carter, declared: "I never wrote a Nick Carter story I would be ashamed to read to a Bible class."

Cover of the first issue of the new *Life* magazine,
November 23, 1936

In the twenties came *Western Story Magazine, Love Story
Magazine,* and Mr. Bernarr Macfadden's *True Story Magazine, True Romances, True Proposals, True Lovers.* Sex
had reared its beautiful ugly head, and *True Confessions*
reached a circulation of 2 million. The stories, though
titilating and very questionably "true," were technically
on the side of innocence. As the years went on, however,
American acceptance of the sordid and the nasty (there
are no other honest words for it) became one of the modern

facts of life. We have seen the growth of "rumor" magazines, which are beneath contempt, and dozens of "confession" magazines which really mean to Tell All, within the limits of police action—*Medical Confessions, Lowdown, Whisper*. Their nearest neighbor is the kind of movie which capitalizes both on horror and sex: *A Werewolf in a Girls' Dormitory*. Everyday life in our decade includes what faces you on any drugstore magazine rack.

As the century went on, changes in the better magazines paralleled the changes in books. Fiction became franker, more realistic, usually more honest. But fiction became displaced progressively by articles reflecting an interest in current social, national and international problems of pressing importance. Such magazines as the *Atlantic Monthly* and *Harper's* have become brisker and brighter and more provocative, streamlined for the modern age. Articles are shorter, for the *Reader's Digest* has cast its condensed shadow over much contemporary writing; and today he who runs may read. New kinds of magazines have emerged, notably the news magazine which encapsulates the week's happenings, again in vivacious form. Picture magazines like *Life* and *Look* have created new perspectives in photojournalism, with their careful layering of news story, reproductions of great art, and "cheesecake." Science and its marvels have become so fascinating—fearfully so sometimes—that the new discoveries in physics, astronomy, and engineering strike one almost with the impact of newspaper headlines. *The Scientific American,* which had a hundred-year-old history as a kind of "popular science" magazine, was transformed into a quality magazine with articles on genetics and nuclear physics and electronics which were by no means easy reading but which became greatly successful. Americans have moved and changed with their times and with the world they live in.

105

"HELLO CENTRAL,
GIVE ME SANTA CLAUS"

Everybody's Magazine in 1910

There is dispute today among commentators on the social scene as to whether the vast growth in book and magazine sales indicates that Americans are reaching a higher cultural level or simply that more people can read. You can prove almost anything you want to, depending upon which set of statistics you select. Some critics point out that the public stimulates itself on violence and drugs itself with emotional clichés; that the danger is not any overt "immorality" in the mass media, but the sterilization of thought and the bankruptcy of our inner resources. It is true, perhaps, that our minds are not likely to get perverted but that they may very well rot. This point of view is supported by some of the reports on our national reading habits. A survey made in 1955 by the American Institute of Public Opinion revealed that only 17 percent of the adults questioned were reading books at the time. In England the percentage was 55 percent. Fifty-seven percent of our high school and 26 percent of our college graduates had not read a single book for the past year. And what kinds of books *had* been read the pollsters evidently did not dare inquire after! One remembers the man in the cartoon in the *Saturday Review,*

A selection from magazine racks in 1964

saying grimly to the clerk in the bookstore: "I don't want anything that affects my thinking!"

The cultural level would not seem to have improved much in recent years. In 1963 a similar survey showed that only 16 percent of the American adults questioned knew of a recently published book they would like to read, though 46 percent claimed that during the last year they had read a book all the way through. All this is depressing enough. But another nationwide survey in 1959 found two out of three American teen-agers "currently reading a book" other than a schoolbook—thus outreading the adult population four to one. Teen-agers even buy books: 26 percent reported buying a book, either paperbound or hard-cover, during the preceding 30 days. And certainly some people, somewhere, are buying over half a billion dollar's worth of books in the United States each year. Buying, and presumably reading, for one does not leave a paperbound book, at least, on the coffee table to impress visitors.

It is improbable that the best books will ever find a mass audience. To anyone interested, however, in the total environment of a people, what they read—sermons and romance, history and science fiction—brings him close to the experiences of a wide variety of minds.

4

The People Sing: Popular
Songs Since 1900

THIS chapter should really be accompanied by an
LP record. But even a discussion of popular
songs drags with it whole areas of connotation which describe better than words, sometimes, the "feel" of a particular time or place.

What songs do you find yourself singing in the shower
these mornings? Not, I imagine, "A Bird in a Gilded Cage,"
or "After the Ball," or "Oh You Spearmint Kiddo with the
Wrigley Eyes," or "Next to Your Mother Who Do You
Love?" But you might well hum songs just as old or older:
"Carry Me Back to Old Virginny," "Let Me Call You
Sweetheart," or even "The Band Played On"—"Casey
would waltz with his strawberry blonde . . ." If you were
of a certain vintage you might have discovered yourself
remembering all the words to "Avalon," "Whispering," or
"A Pretty Girl Is Like a Melody"—or even (just to prove
that not *all* good songs were written in the 1920's) "The
Last Time I Saw Paris," or "Oh, What a Beautiful Morning."

The point is, the tune would be singable or hummable,
and you might be thinking: "They don't write them like

that any more!" If what one hears over the airwaves or from the jukeboxes is any indication, you would be nearly right. I'm not so sure that the philosophy of the lyrics (to use a five-dollar phrase) is much better in the older songs ("Mammy, Mammy, my heart-strings are tangled around Alabamy," or "Whispering While I Cuddle Near You") than in the more modern ones ("Why, Baby, Why don't you treat me like you used to do?"). But if one depended upon sophisticated or intelligent lyrics, his repertoire for shower-singing would be limited. "Put your arms around me, honey, hold me tight" may be elemental, but so are most popular songs of whatever era.

If we look at some of the representative songs of 1900, and some later ones, we can ask to what extent one can interpret a culture through its songs. I say "representative songs," for you can prove anything you like if you pick the right pieces. "God Bless America" and "I Git Along Without You Very Well" were *both* hits of 1939! Yet one does get a sense of change of mood and manners, and also some sense of continuity.

In the early years of the century, families were gathering around the piano and singing songs out of the nineteenth century which are still sung today wherever our people sing: the classics of our song literature, "My Old Kentucky Home," "The Battle Hymn of the Republic," "Goodnight, Ladies." The piano might have been a Beckwith Home Favorite Piano with mandolin attachment, right out of the Sears, Roebuck catalog for $89, which "perfectly reproduces the tones of the mandolin, harp, zither, guitar, banjo, etc." All this if your ear was not too discriminating; the catalog protected itself by saying that "the tone is always a matter of taste." A player piano (Pianola) cost $250 but it would play "everything from a Chopin nocturne to the latest ragtime hit." The family instrument, however, might

Songsheets of the second decade of the twentieth century

just as well have been a Golden Oak Parlor Organ for $19.90, with carved griffins supporting the keyboard at either end, and a stool with big brass claws on its legs. If it had been a really musical family, someone might have accompanied the singers on "Our Stradivarius Model" violin ($1.95—"Equal in every way to violins sold at twice the price"; there were 11 pages of violins listed in 1905). Or if not a violin, then a guitar named for some American university—a new kind of collegiate rating, incidentally; the "Harvard" sold for $21.45, the "Stanford" for $4.25.

But in addition to the classics they were also singing songs from sheet music right off the presses. Some of these, happily, have never been disinterred since. ("The Mansion of Aching Hearts," "The Letter Edged in Black," or "Don't Go Down in the Mine, Father—Dreams Very Often Come

ANYBODY CAN PLAY ANYTHING

SIMPLEX
PIANO PLAYER

Music in the home, 1903

True.") Others, however, have become classics in their turn. On the more serious side, few writers have gone as far with a few songs as Carrie Jacobs Bond with "A Perfect Day," "I Love You Truly," and "Just A-Wearyin' for You" (1901) —all of which earned her a fortune. Ethelbert Nevin's "The Rosary" had just the right combination of love and religion to become a household and concert staple for years. On the lighter side were "In My Merry Oldsmobile" (1905), "In the Good Old Summertime" (1901), "Sweet Adeline" (1903), "School Days" (1907), "Down by the Old Mill

Stream" (1910), "Let Me Call You Sweetheart" (1911), and "Mother Machree" (1910). Here is the stuff which is standard for hundreds of chapters of the Society for the Preservation and Encouragement of Barber Shop Quartet Singing in America. They seem like relics of a simpler, sweeter day when love, which was popular even then, was no less directly sentimental but seemed to depend less upon exclusiveness of possession or upon a passion which burns and consumes.

One must remember, however, that banality was no invention of our day. The nineteen-hundreds could be just as maudlin, and almost as illiterate, as the later Tin Pan Alley. Thus "Just Tell Them That You Saw Me"; the little child's lament "Hello, Central, Give Me Heaven" (1901)—"for my father's there"; "A Bird in a Gilded Cage" (1900)— "And her beauty was sold for an old man's gold"; "The Curse of an Aching Heart" (1913)—"You made me what I am today; I hope you're satisfied!" Even then such ditties must have seemed ridiculous to many. A very popular burlesque of these absurdities was the 1909 "Heaven Will Protect the Working Girl"—"You may tempt the upper classes with your villainous demi-tasses, but Heaven will protect the working girl!" Balancing the rankly sentimental was such a raucously cynical hit as Irving Berlin's early song "My Wife's Gone to the Country, Hurrah! Hurrah!" (1909). "Put on Your Old Grey Bonnet" (1909), still a favorite for group singing, came out about the same time as the disillusioned "I Wonder Who's Kissing Her Now" (1908), and the uninhibited "I Love My Wife, But Oh You Kid" (1909).

Nonsense songs started early, too. Occasionally one has had great popularity, from "Ja-Da" (1918) to "Yes, We Have No Bananas" (1923) to "The Music Goes Round

A song Al Jolson made popular, 1918

and Round" (1935) to "Flat-Foot Floogey with the Floy Floy" (1938). Most of these could be *sung*, however. What does one do with a later song like "I Tot I Taw a Puddy Tat"?

As life in America speeded up, waltzes disappeared into ragtime and ragtime into jazz. People cavorted around dance floors (songs were made to dance to) to Turkey Trots and Bunny Hugs and Camel Walks, and later, to all possible variations of the fox-trot. The songs reflected the change in tempo. The "transportation" song for ex-

114

The automobile outlasted the song.

ample, was no longer "My Merry Oldsmobile" but "Come, Josephine, in My Flying Machine" (1910). Songs of the Old South (usually written then, as they were both earlier and later, by white men who had never been below the Mason-Dixon line) were no longer "The Swanee River" but "Swanee" as belted out by Al Jolson (1918). Instead of basking in "The Sunshine of Your Smile" (1915) the song-writers exclaimed "Oh Johnny, Oh Johnny, How You Can Love!" (1917). The nostalgia of "Shine On, Harvest Moon"

115

(1908) gave way to the lively syncopation of Irving Berlin's "Alexander's Ragtime Band" (1911) and "The Darktown Strutters' Ball" (1917).

When World War I came along it proved to be a singing war, as contrasted with World War II, which seemed much less romantic and produced almost no good songs (one of the few popular ones was stolen from the enemy: "Lili Marlene"). But in 1917 and 1918 soldiers under Y.M.C.A. song leaders, as well as the folks at home in their community sings, were keeping up their spirits with "Over There" (the most popular of all), "Pack Up Your Troubles," "Keep the Home Fires Burning," "Tipperary," "Good Morning, Mr. Zip-Zip-Zip," and "Oh! How I Hate to Get Up in the Morning." Humor was served with "K-K-K-Katy," and perhaps with "Would you rather be a Colonel with an eagle on your shoulder, or a private with a Chicken on your Knee?" Rank sentimentality, with "Hello, Central, Give Me No-Man's Land." The most popular songs of World War II were those which made no direct reference to the conflict, like the nostalgic "I'll Be Seeing You" ("in all the old familiar places")—a good song, as was "The Last Time I Saw Paris," but they were not exactly war songs.

In the nineteen-twenties, which has been called "the golden decade" of the popular song, jazz, still preserving recognizably the melody and rhythmic line of its tunes, even in the midst of syncopation, had not yet turned into swing or "hot" jazz. Those who wanted to could still sing the words and the music, though presumably not many wanted to sing the topical song of 1921, written on the occasion of Caruso's death: "They Wanted a Songbird in Heaven, So God Took Caruso Away." But people *were* singing, in these golden years of the twenties, such songs as "Avalon," "Whispering," "Margie," "April Showers," "Carolina in the Morning," "Three O'Clock in the Morning," "Who?," "Tea for

116

Early automobiles were popular themes for songs.

Two," "My Heart Stood Still," "Bye, Bye, Blackbird," "Button Up Your Overcoat," "Carolina Moon," and "Tip-Toe Through the Tulips."

With the nineteen-thirties, swing and the improvisations of "hot" jazz came in, and the song (whether old or new) tended to become the creature of its arranger or its vocalist. The tune was simply a starting place for variations. More and more—and this was steadily true as boogie-woogie and bebop and progressive jazz and "cool" jazz followed one another—there was an increasing gap between music to

"Till We Meet Again" was a hit song during World War I.

sing and music to listen to on the radio or phonograph.
But in spite of the identification of many vocalists as "jazz
singers," the true lovers of jazz have always scorned the
popular song. It seems to them unrelated to what they
believe are the almost classical qualities of jazz, with its
emphasis upon improvisation and conflicting rhythms or
polyrhythms. Nevertheless, swing or no swing, some of the
best popular songs appeared in the thirties. Cole Porter,
George Gershwin, Jerome Kern, and Irving Berlin were

A musical number from a 1907 musical show

still composing some of the most singable songs in the popular literature.

The mark of the Depression was upon some of the songs of the thirties which, forgetting love, reflected the despair of the decade or tried to whip up cheerfulness in the face of economic disaster. Thus "Brother, Can You Spare a Dime?," "Who's Afraid of the Big Bad Wolf?," "Life is Just a Bowl of Cherries," and the pull-yourself-up-by-your-bootstraps song, "Happy Days Are Here Again."

From the nineteen-twenties on there grew up a kind of aristocracy of popular music—not quite middlebrow, perhaps, but still "popular" in the sense that it was given a warm reception. It was not written for the contortions and writhings and gaspings of certain teen-agers who, as the decades wore on, mobbed the big-name singers and squealed and swooned in the aisles. It emerged, rather, from the musical show. Theatrical producers knew that the public, if it was going to pay for tickets, would insist on hearing some melodies they could remember after they left the theatre. Rudolf Friml gave them this with *Rose Marie* in 1924, and "The Indian Love Call." Sigmund Romberg was approaching the form of the operetta in *Blossom Time* in 1921—built on the life of Franz Schubert—and in *The Student Prince* in 1924, with its "Deep in My Heart, Dear" and its "Serenade" ("Overhead the moon is beaming"). But it was Kern's *Showboat* in 1927 which integrated lovely music and a reasonable enough plot. "Make Believe," "Why Do I Love You," and particularly "Ol' Man River" were landmarks in the modern song. Thus while the "popular" song of the torch singers and the later whimperers and whiners (the special province of the radio and disc jockey) continued in one direction, the sophistication and maturity and even the musical solidity of the better songs appeared in musical plays. Not musical comedies in the old sense, but plays like Gershwin's *Porgy and Bess* ("I've Got Plenty of Nuthin'," "Summertime," "It Ain't Necessarily So"). And in the forties and fifties in such productions as the Rodgers-Hammerstein *Oklahoma!* (1943). "Oh, What a Beautiful Morning," "People Will Say We're in Love," and "The Surrey with the Fringe on Top" were clearly the best songs of the year. Then *South Pacific* in 1949 and *The King and I* in 1951. And in 1955 the Lerner-Loewe *My Fair Lady,* where George Bernard Shaw and melody and laugh-

Peggy

Words by
HARRY WILLIAMS
Music by
NEIL MORET

60

LEO. FEIST NEW YORK

Folks were singing "Peggy" in 1919.

ter and wit combined to make a monumentally pleasant show, and to produce some of the best songs of our time.

Here, then, have been some of the changes in popular songs over the years. Somehow it is easier to discuss Al Jolson than Elvis Presley or Fabian or Mineo or any of their successors—and it is difficult to say anything about the songs one finds in the Hit Parade or in the song-hit magazines. One thing is sure: the turnover is faster today, and a hit song, instead of being good for a year or two, gets swamped in the flood of new so-called "hits" in three

121

"Ol' Man River," from *Show Boat* in 1925, has become a classic.

months. How does one explain the popular songs of the fifties and sixties? Does anybody *sing* them, except professional vocalists, many of whom couldn't be heard twenty feet away if they couldn't cuddle a microphone?

What does the popular song tell us over the years about the people who sing or listen to them?

Well, we've had Irish songs, and Mother songs—and sometimes both together, as in "That Old Irish Mother of Mine." We've had Moon songs and June songs, and Negro songs. There's an interesting point here, however. The old-

"Bye Bye Blackbird," 1926

time minstrel show could not possibly be revived today; public sensitivities are such that singers have to sing "In the evening by the moonlight you can hear those *chillun* singing"—not, "hear those darkies singing." This is sociologically quite understandable, but censorship takes strange forms sometimes. Not long ago a Congressman of Irish extraction urged a national ban on the song "Who Threw the Overalls in Mrs. Murphy's Chowder?" since it was clearly an insult to the Irish.

We've had rain songs and river songs and cowboy ballads and stamping hillbilly songs (how many of these last since

STANDARD
"I Got To Go Where You Are"
CHLO-E
(Song of the Swamp)
The Lucille Benstead Souvenir Edition
Lyric by
Gus Kahn
Music by
Neil Morét
Villa Morét

"Chlo-e," a 1927 song, may still be heard occasionally.

the early thirties!). We have Dream songs—Dream songs of every description, from "Meet Me Tonight in Dreamland" (1909) to "Have You Ever Seen a Dream Walking?" (1933), to some modern hits, one of which runs: " 'Cause I'm a hog for you, babe, can't get enough of your love; when I go to sleep at night, that's the only thing I'm dreamin' of."

This may not quite be great lyric writing, but it is enough to plunge us into a central consideration: aside from the novelty numbers, 95 percent of the popular songs are variations on a single theme—"I love you." There are many

"Me and My Shadow," 1927

kinds of love, but love in the popular song is always the passionate love of the boy for the girl, or vice versa, based usually upon exclusive and complete possession and intense desire—jealous love, often, or love so pantingly idealized, so "dreamlike," that it has almost no relation to life as it is. (I'm not talking now about the authentic blues song, which faces up to the sometimes miserable conditions of life, or the folk song, which has created its own modern cult, but about Tin Pan Alley songs.)

Within these categories there are many shades of love: love pleading, love lonesome and deserted, love triumphant

("Everybody loves my baby, but my baby don't love nobody but me"); love excited, love recriminatory—but usually love enduring forever in a continuous state of bliss (which fortunately rhymes with "kiss"), and love demanding the ultimate in complete absorption. More frequently than not the lover whinnies in an orgy of self-pity: I'm lonesome, I'm blue, or I need sympathy, or "I Ain't Got Nobody," or "I'm Dancing with Tears in My Eyes," or more recently, "The Big Hurt," and "It's Time to Cry."

A 1931 song of the heyday of Rudy Vallee. Vallee is again a popular entertainer on stage and television.

If people believed what the popular song says to them or felt the way it tells them to feel, an analyst of our social order would have reason to be gloomy. Mr. Hayakawa, the semanticist, makes the point that the idealization of the popular song, the making of impossible demands on life, leads to frustration, and frustration leads to demoralization and despair. Undoubtedly the lyrics of the popular song deal in magic—the witchery of love, its permanence plus its immediate satisfactions which seem to prove its permanence! It is clearly a world of ecstatic or lugubrious unreality.

But I wonder if even its addicts take its irradiated sentiments seriously. The *tune* is—or used to be—the important thing, and the words something to fill in with. People used to sing: "When my baby smiles at me, my heart goes roaming in paradise," but I don't remember that they ever took that as a philosophy of the hereafter. And occasionally words and music do come together with an intelligent-enough resonance, for which we should be happy. There is, I suppose, a danger that the concept of love as projected in the popular song could collaborate with the same image in other media to keep our young people in a protracted emotional adolescence. But one can still have a good deal of faith in the resiliency of American youth, and the ability of most of them to accrete a lot of common sense. They have heard as much about the divorce rate today as about "Love me and the world is mine!" Moreover, I suspect that the teen-ager's devotion to the Hit Parade is as much social as personal; it's music to listen to so that you can talk about it. The devotion to styles of music, too, is ephemeral. Rock 'n' roll at last became unfashionable; not that the currently popular songs, however, are any great improvement.

The magazine *Variety* some time ago gave encouragement to those who would like to see good singable melodies come back again. In 1956, *Variety* listed the top hits of the previous half century, based on everything from originality to sales figures. They were: "In the Shade of the Old Apple Tree," "School Days," "Casey Jones," "Down by the Old Mill Stream," "Let Me Call You Sweetheart," "Alexander's Ragtime Band," "I Want a Girl," "Waiting for the Robert E. Lee," "St. Louis Blues," "Over There," and "God Bless America."

Bing Crosby (was there ever any other singer in the thirties?) brought out an album, not long ago, of "songs to sing at home." The teen-agers have had their fill, he said hopefully, of shoo-bee-do-bee-do, and "my kind of music is coming back. I've lived through fads before." There may be hope yet for those who are tired of what they find in the entrails of the ubiquitous jukebox. The old "community sings" have disappeared in the complexity of life today, but people young and old do still sing, around a campfire or at the service club or in small groups at home. And when they sing they go back, almost perforce, to the older songs. Some parents who can remember the nineteen-twenties were startled when their children rediscovered and passed on as news in the musical world—Al Jolson! Mitch Miller developed a phenomenally successful TV program by inviting anyone who could tune in to "sing along" with the old tunes. Ten of the "Sing Along With Mitch" record albums have sold 4.5 million copies.

Everyday life is constantly meeting up with our past, as well as with tomorrow.

5

The Continuing Revolution:
Science, Invention, Technology

THERE has been no period in the history of the
world in which the everyday lives of human beings have changed as rapidly as in the first half of the
twentieth century. Many of the changes have been created
by scientific and technological achievements so far-reaching
in their total impact that most of our environment is determined by them. Yet such is the force of custom that we
accept them casually as matters of course, seldom stopping
to consider that the electric light and the nylon stocking
are miracles of man's mastery of nature.

Science, technology, manufacture and distribution are
all interlocked in this story of change in the modern world.
The photographic camera or aureomycin did not spring
full-blown from the brain of some inventive genius. Behind
the Kodak there lay, centuries before, the discovery of the
principles of optics and Leonardo da Vinci's description of
the pinhole *camera obscura*. Behind antibiotics was Harvey's
discovery of the circulation of the blood and, later, the
confirmation of the germ theory of disease. Every inventor
stands on the shoulders of the scientists who have preceded
him. The development of his invention, its availability for

everyday use, depends in turn upon a whole related series of technologies involving manufacture, distribution and sale. Gutenberg invented movable type but many things had to happen before *The New York Times* could send facsimile copies electronically for its West Coast edition. It is significant, at the same time, how much of our modern environment depends upon a few basic principles. Invent the internal-combustion engine and crowded highways are inevitable. Discover the working principle of electricity and invent the motor, and the electric toothbrush is just around the corner. Learn that silver salts are sensitive to light and you prepare the way for Cinerama. Invent barbed wire, and the days of the open range in the West are numbered.

It is our task at the moment to explore a few of the impacts that the world of the machine has had upon life since 1900. We have already looked at the automobile; we shall reserve the phonograph, the movies, radio and television for later discussion as instruments, primarily, of entertainment. But there are still areas of great importance left.

Think first of the life of the ordinary town household in 1900 (life in the country was of course still more primitive). The chances were that it was without electricity. It might well have had gas, though the gas range was not introduced until after 1880. This meant that cooking was frequently done on a cast-iron wood or coal range, and the Tuesday ironing was accomplished by means of flatirons heated on the same stove. Toast was made in the oven or over the open fire. All beating or mixing of food was done by hand, as was of course dishwashing. Clothes were scrubbed in tubs, with washboards, unless by chance the household could afford a washing machine which worked by cranking a hand wheel. The standard soap for this was yellow laundry soap—no detergents or even soap flakes.

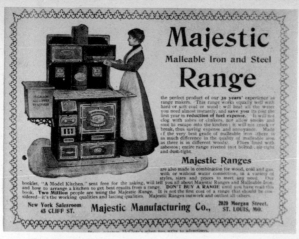

The latest in cooking stoves in 1901

Rugs were swept either with a broom or a hand carpet sweeper. Food was kept cool in summer in an ice-refrigerator, usually an upright box with two compartments. The upper compartment would hold a foot-square cake of ice plus butter and other perishables, while the lower compartment held the balance of the perishable food. One cake of ice might serve for as much as a week before needing replacement. Father shaved with a straight-edge razor, and mother sewed on a foot-treadle sewing machine. On Saturday night you took a bath in an enameled cast-iron claw-footed tub that had been recently installed when a small sewing room had been converted into a bathroom. Even in the 1880's five out of six houses in American cities had no bathtubs.

There were rumors in 1900 of easier times ahead, but even then people were wondering if electricity would ever replace gas. An electric kitchen had been exhibited at the Columbian World Fair in 1893—not yet a stove, for every utensil, such as saucepan, broiler, water heater, had its own outlet. Not until 1896 at Buffalo, New York, was the first large-scale electric generating plant erected. Voltages had not yet been standardized.

When the break came, however, it seemed to come very

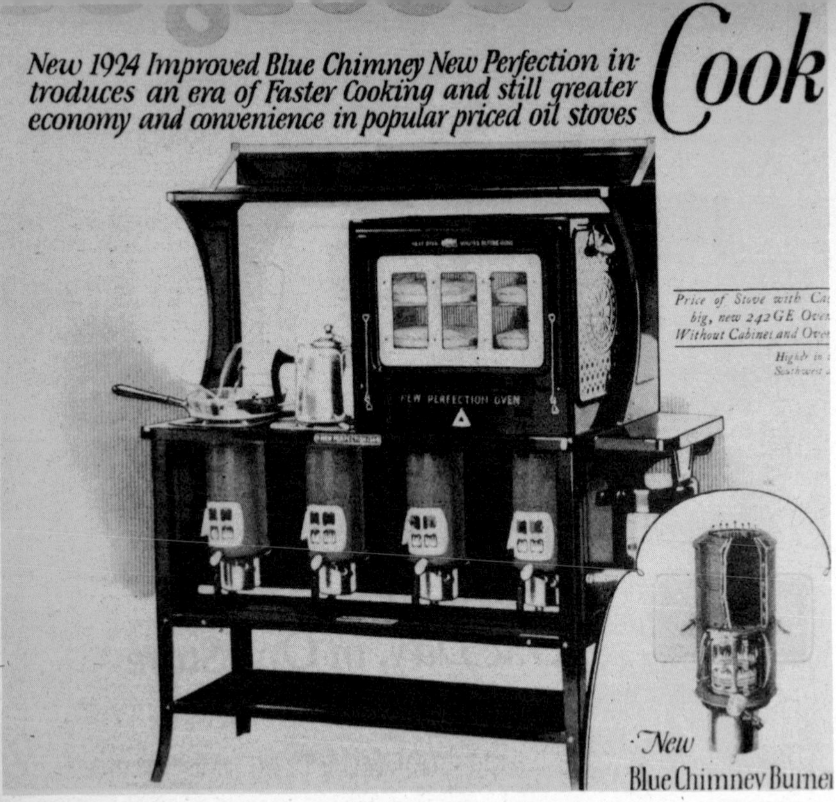

Cook

Price of Stove with Ca
big, new 242 GE Oven
Without Cabinet and Ove

Highly in
Southwest

New
Blue Chimney Burner

Oil stoves were still being used in 1924.

fast, though mechanization did not fully invade the domestic sphere until after World War I. The production of enameled washbasins and bathtubs actually doubled in the United States between 1921 and 1923. The wiring of houses for electricity was the major revolution, with all its high costs and dubious efficiency. In 1906 the Westinghouse Co. began to advertise the electric iron; by 1909 the Hoover Co. was running full-page ads for vacuum cleaners in the *Saturday Evening Post*. The vacuum cleaner entered the mail-order catalogs in 1917—final proof of its success— though the advertisements still had to preach its labor-saving delights: "No raising of dust—it's a pleasure to use." The electric refrigerator was not sold by Sears, Roebuck until 1932. In 1923 there were only 20,000 refrigerators in the whole country. By 1941 there were 3.5 million, and in 1963

General Electric's first electric range in 1906 contained thirteen appliances—including coffee maker, toaster, and waffle iron—and required thirty switches and plugs.

An electric kitchen of the 1960's

well over 4 million were *manufactured*. Ice, except as made in such refrigerators, became a disappearing commodity.

The statistics are astounding. In 1912 only 2.4 million dollars' worth of electrical household appliances of all kinds were sold; in 1929, $160 million; in 1963 over $9,000,000,-000. Electric ranges and washing machines quadrupled between 1940 and 1963; electric dishwashers and clothes driers quadrupled between 1950 and 1963. And all sorts of machines and appliances never dreamed of by anyone before World War I were sweeping the market: air conditioners (11,000 sold in 1940; 2 million in 1963); electric blankets (800,000 in 1950; 5.5 million in 1963). Also electric shavers (which sextupled 1940–1963), electric mixers and beaters, electric shoe buffers, electric vibrators, hedge shears, ironers, coffee grinders, can openers, toasters, grills, coffeepots. You name it and someone will attach a motor to it.

Most important of all, perhaps—and the first to appear —was the electric light, developed for practical use in the United States by Thomas A. Edison. One does not say "invented," for others had brought the incandescent light to laboratory perfection about the same time as Edison. (Inventions, incidentally, seem to have a habit of coming into the minds of widely separated inventors simultaneously. Three sewing machines came on the market about the time that Elias Howe developed his model. Motion-picture photography appeared in Europe concurrently with Edison's experiments in the United States.) But Edison, though no genius in pure science, was an inspired tinkerer; he could make things work. He won his eminence through the combination of hard work and native ingenuity which Americans have always prized. He was an inventor in the shrewd, commonsense, Yankee way, belonging to the cut-and-fit school—at least this was the impression he liked to give. In an industrial age Edison, like Henry Ford, became a symbol of the American Way for many people.

Edison started to manufacture electric incandescent bulbs in 1880, fragile carbon-filament lamps burning with a rosy glow which at the time seemed devastatingly brilliant. About the same time, as a necessary corollary, he built dynamos, and in 1882 the Edison Electric Illuminating Co. of New York started operation, supplying 59 customers having a total of 1,284 outlets. The tungsten-filament lamp, nearly three times as efficient as the carbon lamp, came into production in 1907. Before many years transmission lines crisscrossed the countryside and light was available to any American who could turn a switch or press a button. Nevertheless as late as 1910 the General Electric Co. felt it had

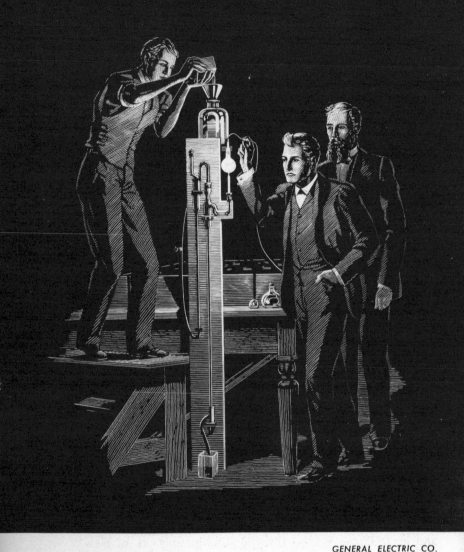

Edison lighting his first incandescent lamp. It burned for forty hours.

to advertise "thirty reasons for using electric light." Among them were these benefits: "odorless, sootless, fumeless, explosionless, signifies success, frightens thieves, consumes no oxygen."

If one wanted to describe in a phrase the major components of change in American life in the twentieth century he could say that our civilization rides on rubber but is supported by electric power. The skyscraper itself, the very emblem of the U.S.A. to many foreigners, would be inconceivable without the electric elevator (first used in 1892) and the telephone.

The telephone in turn epitomizes the whole system of mass communication without which an industrial age would fall apart. Patented by Alexander Graham Bell in 1876–77 (here again there were disputes about priority), the first telephone switchboard was installed in New Haven in 1878, with 8 lines and 21 subscribers. Today there are over 85 million telephones carrying over 300 million daily conversations.

The broad mechanization of the modern household has

Edison, Burroughs, Ford, and Firestone—all pioneers of modern industry—on a camping trip in 1918

worked its own social changes—or more accurately, perhaps, it has cushioned the effects of social changes already in progress. Even in 1900, magazines were running articles on "the servant problem," and the virtual abolition of the permanent servant class is an accepted fact of life today. The former "hired girl" now works as a beautician or assembles transistors in an electronics factory. Hence the eager acceptance by the housewife of labor-saving devices and the rise of huge businesses to supply her electrical and mechanical needs. Everything has been done that could be done for her aesthetic satisfaction as well as her physical comfort. Industrial designers have worked to make beautiful the necessary household implements. The visible mechanism has disappeared from sight. Everything from the washing machine to the iron to the toaster is "streamlined"—a word which originally meant a reduction of wind resistance but now implies merely graceful design. It is even applied to the bathtub, one of the chief virtues of which, as someone has pointed out, is its immobility. The housewife today doing her work in her kitchen laboratory (which is tinted in becoming colors) lives in a happy mechanical world which is frequently not even isolated from the rest of the house. The wife-mother-cook-maid looks in one direction over a counter into the rumpus room where the children play, and in the other into the dining area which is itself a corner of the living room.

The modern mechanization of life, with its conveniences and its sometimes depressing standardizations, has reached even the food that comes out of that kitchen. At the turn of the century one could still buy cornmeal, crackers, prunes, or pickles out of a barrel, but the art of packaging, with its guarantee of cleanliness and convenience, was becoming common. Cheese was still cut from the wheel, to be sure, and it was real cheese, not a processed substitute.

Most housewives made their own bread and it was real bread, not baked in a soggy, spongy uniformity or from flour first robbed of essential ingredients and then "enriched" and "fortified" by the addition of vitamins and minerals. If the housewife baked a cake she mixed her own batter, rather than pouring milk into a packaged preparation of flour and powdered eggs. It is true, however, that nowhere in those early years did she have access to the bewildering array of tempting foods, fresh or canned, which one finds today as a matter of course on the shelves of any neighborhood market. By way of compensation, perhaps, the "TV dinner" was still unthought of.

Yet few things have added more to the ease of food preparation in the home than the development of the quick-freezing process, patented in 1925 by Clarence Birdseye and introduced to the public in 1928. Under this process vegetables, fruits, and orange juice tasted much better than canned goods. Soon, too, meats of all kinds were being frozen. The consumption of frozen food products grew enormously: 39 million pound-cartons in 1934; 600 million in 1944; over 10,000,000,000 in 1962, including 5,500,000,000 pounds of citrus juices, most of it being orange or grapefruit. Eventually the freezer or freezer-refrigerator became standard equipment in many homes.

Since 1906, too, the consumer has had a much better chance of buying uncontaminated food from his grocer and butcher. Until then the adulteration and the unhygienic preparation of food for sale had been unregulated; one took his chances of ingesting putrid or decomposed animal or vegetable substances in whatever he bought. Foods were coated, or colored with dangerous dyes to hide deterioration or the use of inferior materials. The muckraking school of journalism began to uncover some of the more cynically irresponsible practices in the early years of the century, and

Upton Sinclair's novel *The Jungle,* in 1906, alarmed and horrified the nation. It was an exposé of the meat-packing industry. People learned that their beef and pork products might well contain bits of ground rat and all kinds of refuse, and public clamor finally forced the passage of the Pure Food and Drug Act of 1906. This, with its subsequent amendments, assured the purchaser that his food would be properly inspected and labeled, and prepared under reasonably sanitary conditions.

The act also controlled some of the wilder aberrations of the huge patent medicine industry, which not only had claimed incredible cures for its noxious compounds but had traditionally used opium and its derivatives as standard pain-killers and pacifiers. Tons of almost pure alcohol, colored and flavored, were sold as remedies under hundreds of different labels whose curative claims were limited only by the imaginations of the manufacturers. One of the big sellers at the turn of the century was Peruna, presented chiefly as a cure for catarrh. It sold for one dollar, and consisted of half a pint of alcohol, a pint and a half of water, some pepper, and burnt sugar for color. In 1906 the total sales of patent medicines in the United States reached $180 million. In 1905 the Sears, Roebuck catalog had 20 pages of nostrums and patent medicines. In 1915, however, there was only one page devoted to medicines, and none of them was a miracle cure.

Even today, however, it is instructive to read on food labels the fine print which, by law, lists the ingredients in the package. Pre-

Typical ad for a patent remedy before 1906

A scare ad of 1901

sumably none of the additives to insure uniformity of color or texture, to lengthen shelf life, or to replace necessary dietary components which had been taken from the original food is harmful to health. But there is a formidable, and for the consumer an impenetrable array of dyes, emulsifiers, stabilizers, and thickeners in the most common foods—caseinates, monoglycerides, diglycerides, polyexyethylenes and sorbitan monooleates, to name only a few that appear in ice cream. If you buy packaged raisins and breakfast foods you may well get an inclusion of hydroxyanisole. If you chew gum, you get not only chicle, but under the cloak of "gum base" and "softeners" you may receive some 25 other ingredients from massaranduba balata to butadiene-styrene rubber to propyl gallate. The Food and Drug Administration assures us that none of these hurts the digestive tract. It is curious, however, that it seems to take the public outrage which is aroused after people have been blinded by an eyelash cosmetic or killed by an elixir containing dangerous amounts of sulfa to precipitate such a revision of the law as occurred in 1938—or in 1962 in connection with the child-deforming drug thalidomide. The hazards as well as the blessings of modern technology enfold our everyday life.

But nowhere has twentieth-century science succeeded more triumphantly than in medicine. The nineteenth century saw the discovery of the germ theory of disease and the initial development of vaccines and antitoxins to cure hydrophobia and diphtheria. In 1895 50 percent of the children who caught diphtheria died; within five years the mortality fell to twelve percent and has diminished ever since. The antibacterial powers of penicillin, discovered partly by accident by Sir Alexander Fleming in 1929, were established by 1941, and the therapeutic value of sulfanilimide had been confirmed in the United States in 1936. Since then the multiplication and use of the various antibiotics (streptomycin, chloromycetin, aureomycin, terramycin, tetracycline, and many others) has meant that almost half of all medical treatment includes the use of one of them. Such killers as syphilis, tuberculosis, meningitis, typhoid fever, pneumonia, and polio have been subdued. The incidence of death from such diseases decreased 80 percent between 1943 and 1962. By 1965, deaths from polio were almost entirely eliminated. Other boons for the diagnosis and treatment of disease came with radium and the X ray. Madame Curie had discovered radium in 1899, Roentgen the X ray in 1895. Both are now main instruments of therapy.

All this is reflected both in the decreasing death rate since 1900 (from 17.2 to 9.5 per thousand people) and in the increase of life expectancy at birth. The child born in 1900 had a life expectancy of only 48.2 years; in 1950, 65.5 years; and in 1962, 70 years. For the first time within the memory of man the problems of old age—economic, medical, cultural—have become a national concern.

The "wonder drugs" have been made possible, as far as large-scale production is concerned, by the development of chemical science and its ability to synthesize organic compounds. This creation-by-synthesis is not only true of medicine but is responsible for thousands of objects which are very much a part of our daily lives. The science of plastics and the proliferation of their use is perhaps the most pervasive index of technological change since 1900, when

"Before and after" ad of 1901

celluloid collars and hairbrushes and photographic film
seemed the last word in scientific achievement.

As I sit in a plastic-covered chair at this plastic-covered
desk which is painted with plastic paint, I wear eyeglasses
with plastic frames, plastic tie, socks, shirt, and shirt buttons, and smoke a plastic-stemmed pipe which I light with
a plastic lighter. I have at hand plastic tape, plastic glue,
a plastic radio in a plastic cabinet, and a plastic telephone.
At lunch I shall eat from plastic dishes on a plastic table-
cloth, drink milk poured from a plastic container into a
plastic glass, and eat bread extracted from a plastic wrapper.

Later I shall brush my teeth with a plastic toothbrush and go to bed on a plastic mattress, to be wakened later by a plastic alarm clock. No one of these artifacts—and there are thousands of them—was known in 1900. If I wanted to name them I should have to use such words as Bakelite, Nylon, Dacron, Teflon, Plexiglas, Koroseal, Vinyl. I am immersed in plastics, and they still seem a kind of alchemy.

It all started with the invention of Bakelite by L. H. Baekeland about 1909. People were familiar with the magic of coal-tar products isolated by chemical analysis, largely by the Germans before World War I—dyes, perfumes, disinfectants, fertilizers, explosives. But the new science of synthesis created useful materials by bringing together their constituent parts. Bakelite was made from phenol formaldehyde under heat and pressure and was a hard, insoluble solid, resistant to acids and heat, non-shrinking and machinable. Baekeland's first commercial success was with electrical insulators but soon the material was adapted to hundreds of other uses, and before long other wizards of the laboratory developed other kinds of plastics. One heard them grouped as phenolic, urea, acrylic, cellulose. The latter was the base for many early plastics. Cellophane was first manufactured by Dupont in 1923, and when viscose yarn under the name of rayon began to appear on the market in 1924, the sale of silk stockings started to dwindle. The 1937 rayon production was six times greater than that of silk. In 1934 Dupont came up with nylon, a fiber much better for most uses than rayon, though it did not reach the domestic market in quantity until after World War II. Scientists had learned to hook molecules together to form giant ones called polymers with new physical properties— tough, hard, or resilient. They could be made to resemble wood, leather, or rubber, and in many instances they were superior to the originals they imitated. These complex

144

molecular arrangements could be created almost on order to fulfill any described need. In 1920 the United States produced 5 million pounds of synthetic plastics of all kinds; in 1930, about 50 million; and in 1960 some 4,000 fabricators of plastic and resin materials shipped products worth $1,800,000,000.

The difference between the origin of Bakelite and, say, Dacron was symptomatic of a change that had come over large-scale industrial development as the century progressed. Bakelite was the invention of one man; the newer plastics were the result of *team* research (and thus anonymous) in the laboratories of huge industrial organizations. The place of the entrepreneur in American technology was disappearing. No longer could a man, working in his garage, invent and market a plastic or an automobile or a radio tube. All this became a part of massive concentration in companies with large funds for research and development, and with the capital to exploit the products once they were ready for the market. Something of the old freewheeling individualism had vanished in the highly mechanized American scene. Many benefits accrued from this: cheapness, through mass production, and a decrease in the span of time between the initial invention and its appearance in the retail store. Something also may have been lost, but the fact is that it is the great corporation which molds the American economy in our time, and floods the market with new products. It has been estimated that every ten years the amount of scientific effort doubles. The head of a major electronics concern pointed out in 1962 that 90 percent of his company's profits came from products which had not been on the market ten years before.

To describe fully the industrial changes which have shaped our daily lives would require more space than we

have here. As always, it is an interlocking series of activities. It is in large part a function of mass production, which in turn hinges on the assembly line and upon the development of machine tools which can perform automatically and accurately the complicated processes necessary to mass production. These tools in their turn awaited the invention of electronic controls utilizing the principle of the feedback, which with superhuman accuracy telegraphs to the machine what it should do at each stage of its operation, and how it can correct its mistakes. Gradually automation has taken over the work of many men; it is seen at its most efficient peak, perhaps, in such an operation as the continuous functioning of a huge oil-cracking plant, controlled by a very few men who watch meters and occasionally push a button.

Ads that appealed to vanity, as at left and above, were just a little more bizarre in 1904 than some advertisements of today.

And as always in technological revolutions, automation, with its resulting unemployment, has become a social as well as an industrial problem.

There are other developments in science which do not cross the daily paths of most people but which have, in their totality, a lasting impact on the human mind. I don't mean the specter of the A-bomb, or the mysteries of space travel, which is a fairy story of its own, but such wonders as the electron microscope and the great new telescopes. The former, magnifying to hundreds of thousands of diameters, can make protein molecules or viruses stand out like players on a football field. At the other extreme, the 200-inch telescope on Mount Palomar has taught us that our own galaxy of the Milky Way has 30,000,000,000 suns, each with its own planets, and that our galaxy is only one of 1,000,000,-

147

000 or so. In 1960 it photographed a pair of colliding galaxies at a distance of 4,700,000,000 light-years—the farthest optical penetration ever made into space. More recently the radar telescope, with its gathering field of 250 feet instead of 200 inches, has caught radio waves emitted by stars beyond the range of any conceivable optical telescope. The mind can accept such extensions into space but can't really begin to comprehend them; there is still room for mystery.

The scientific and technological achievements of the last half century have introduced Americans to what they like to think of as an economy of abundance—not for everyone, to be sure, but for most people. As a whole we are healthier and wealthier, better housed and fed, and certainly more gadgetized than our counterparts of 1900. Yet an industrial civilization has to do more than make goods; it has to sell them, and here the story of national advertising becomes important.

Certainly advertising is almost as close to us today as our skins; it shrieks at us relentlessly from every loudspeaker, every billboard, every magazine and newspaper— even from the sky, sometimes. One gets anesthetized to much of it, but a market director recently estimated that the average American family, during a normal 15-hour day of commuting, newspaper and magazine reading, and TV viewing, is exposed to 1,518 advertisements. What kind of an image does this give one of American life, and how has advertising changed over the years?

The average consumer, as he appears in the ads, is young, for Americans tend to adore youth. He is happy, healthy, active, good-looking, and of course financially able to buy the Product. He is happy in large part because he has discovered the delights of what the advertiser has to sell. If he has a sour stomach or closed pores or nagging headaches

A distinguished tobacco chewer, 1914

it is because he has not yet heard about the reliefs that await him. The cigarette always tastes right, the beer is always the world's finest, the car-rental service always catapults you easily into the driver's seat. The automobile gives you "total performance"; the milk of magnesia brings you on-the-spot relief; the mattress is a dream, not a nightmare. And people don't really have to work anymore—mother just stands around in an immaculate housedress and pushes buttons. We are an optimistic, buoyant, cheery race of people, with brows unfurrowed by worry or even by thought, for we are so busy being *consumers.*

All this is no invention of the nineteen-sixties. Generations ago people were haggard—in the ads—for want of the right nerve tonic or beauty cream, or jubilant because they were wearing the right shoes. But as one leafs through the ads of the early century he notices a curious matter-of-

This food ad of 1901 was "cute," while . . .

factness about most of them. If they urge the purchase of soap it is because it gets you clean, not because it gives you the bloom of a new and undiscovered beauty. As we have seen, the manufacturers of automobiles had the curious idea that the reader was interested in the stability of his car as much as in its sleek looks, and wanted to know how easily the magneto could be replaced. In 1917 the Oakland Sensible Six was advertised only as "thoroughly practical." Piper Heidsieck Chewing Tobacco, to be sure, had a "champagne flavor"—an obvious snob appeal. (When, one wonders, did the last Mail Pouch Chewing Tobacco sign cover

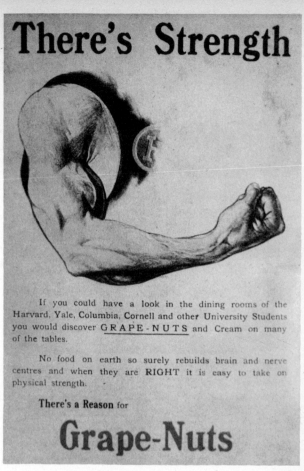

There's Strength

If you could have a look in the dining rooms of the Harvard, Yale, Columbia, Cornell and other University Students you would discover GRAPE-NUTS and Cream on many of the tables.

No food on earth so surely rebuilds brain and nerve centres and when they are RIGHT it is easy to take on physical strength.

There's a Reason for

Grape-Nuts

. . . this food ad of 1906 appealed to vanity.

the side of whose barn?) Steinway pianos may have been the "instrument of the immortals," but Paris Garters simply held your socks up, and toothpaste didn't pretend to do anything but clean your teeth. Universal Varnish even thought it could sell paint by quoting John Ruskin! Later on, General Motors dipped into Ruskin, too; in 1924 it quoted him as saying "There is no wealth but life," which seemed, somehow, to include automobiles.

By 1910, to be sure, Grape-Nuts was getting into high gear by relieving "mental dullness," and the doctor's en-

The "cute" device at left sold biscuits in 1902, while the "corn" at the right sold cornflakes.

dorsement had been used. But in 1914, Listerine was living in an innocent world, for it was simply "an agreeable antiseptic solution for the mouth." Some of the ads were coy or cute and some patent medicine ads astonishingly descriptive (in terms of today's evasions). But most of them assumed that all they had to do was to tell you that here was a good product, cheap.

With the nineteen-twenties the pressure began to be stepped up. You began to buy values, not commodities; dreams, not things. The glamorousness of romantic beauties in idyllic settings began to be emphasized. Perfume no longer, to paraphrase a modern ad, would "make you smell good, like a lady should," but held out promises of mystery, gaiety, challenge, seductiveness. Listerine would now make you acceptable socially and became in the ads the remedy for the newly invented disease halitosis and the ideal deodorant, to be used "some day when you don't have time for a tub or a shower." Some ads tried to bully the reader: If your wife won't speak to you in the car going home from the party you'd better buy that book of etiquette. Some tried to frighten the consumer: Four out of five have pyorrhea, and almost anyone could have Paralyzed Pores or Ashtray Breath or Intestinal Toxicity or Colon Collapse. Most of these ads were slanted to make you believe that you could have success in love if you obeyed the advertiser and used his product. Soon the day of the miracle ingredient was at hand, and D72, Puralin, or Irium would save you from unspeakable disaster. Advertisers had not yet learned to conduct "motivational" researches, with batteries of psychologists to tell them the consumer's weakest points of resistance, but the Hard Sell was on the way.

In the simpler days before radio or TV all you had to do was to close the magazine to shut out the Message. Now you meet it at every turn; in your living room it shouts at you with diabolical iteration. Against the decency and dignity of many ads you have to set the vulgar, breathlessly affected, brutally noisy, or frighteningly imbecile attacks upon your senses. The fearful thing about all this is that it *sells products,* and thus would seem to be its own justification.

It has been pointed out by informed observers that advertising is the backbone of our economy, and on that basis one can have no objection to it in principle. The art of advertising, frequently, lies in making luxuries seem like necessities. If the economy is to expand we must make more

153

things to buy; hence national prosperity depends upon your acquiring not just what you need but what you think you would like to have. One method of convincing you of this is the device of "psychological obsolescence," which shows you that the hair dryer or dishwasher which has been serving you well should be turned in for a new model which has round corners and pink handles. This is the economy of abundance—a spiral which can end only when everyone has no new material needs (unthinkable) or when he has no money with which to satisfy them (thinkable). The possibility of this latter dilemma has been cushioned, however, by the device of installment buying. It was used early in the century by Sears, Roebuck and others but since then has become a national habit. It is a Utopia made possible, in large part, by the $14,000,000,000 annual expenditure for advertising. The profession itself supports, directly or indirectly, many people. Thus do we live in each other's pockets.

And as we shall see, the massive advances in science and technology in the twentieth century have changed not only the ways in which people work and think, but also the ways in which they entertain themselves—or more accurately, perhaps, allow themselves to be entertained.

6

Entertainment

THE families of 1900 had no automobiles, no movies, no radio or TV, no hi-fi sets. Yet somehow in spite of this they managed to enjoy themselves, not having had the foresight to regret the absence of what no one had ever heard of. As a matter of fact, few people (except the so-called idle rich, who were often busy themselves) had great amounts of leisure. Husbands worked long hours at office, store, factory, or farm; wives, without laundromats or vacuum cleaners, found it full-time work just to keep the house going. Even so, people had some time to read and to engage in many family activities, as well as to do a good deal of "visiting" which the tempo of modern life doesn't allow for.

The clue to home life in the early part of the century was that entertainment was usually found *in the home*. People played parlor games, flinch (a card game), bridge (or Authors in stricter houses); they bought game boards for caroms (played with round counters which were snapped by one's finger into corner pockets on a square board), checkers, dominoes, chess. They played ping-pong. Despite the bad odor in which pool halls were held, they sometimes

Home billiard tables were advertised in 1903, just as pool tables are now popular in suburban home basements.

installed a billiard table in the home—though it was quite a trick for a woman to manipulate a cue in the costume of 1903.

Hobbies were as popular then as now, if sometimes different. Men collected stamps or streetcar transfers; boys, picture cards of baseball players; women, buttons. Boys whittled and played with chemical sets or working-model steam engines; girls, with their mothers, painted china or crocheted or embroidered doilies, corset covers, sofa pillows. Sometimes the whole family engaged in an activity of which one can still find relics in dusty attics: woodburning, or "pyrography," to give it its aristocratic name. For some years this was a great fad, and households were adorned with blackly etched collar-button boxes, necktie holders, jardiniere stands. All the family could enjoy, too, what was theoretically for the children: the magic lantern. It was powered by acetylene gas produced by a hissing carbide generator, and it cast on a sheet wonderful pictures from colored-glass slides which held all the marvels of the world. *The Youth's Companion* advertised such views as "Darius Green and His Wonderful Flying Machine" (comic); "John Gilpin's Ride" (ditto); vistas of New York City, London, Paris, Constantinople, and St. Petersburg. Some machines even had dissolving views.

If the family could spend a little more, the newfangled phonograph—Edison, Victor, Columbia—was a source of great amazement and delight. Thomas Edison had invented the device in 1877 and in the early years of the century it was being promoted vigorously. In thousands of homes it was belching out through a tin horn, from a wax cylinder or disc, mechanical-acoustic noises dimly representing the

A 1909 woodburning set

A postcard projector of 1909

world of sound. The frequency range was small, but just to hear it at all was a marvel. In 1905 you were invited to lean back and listen to "Vaudeville at Home with the Edison Phonograph"—comic songs, coon songs, specialties such as "The Professor and the Musical Tramp," the "Rube Talking Specialty," and "Courtin' Melinda." You heard banjo solos, piccolo solos, cornet trios, bell solos, tenor solos ("Bright Eyes, Good Bye"), hymns ("Rescue the Perishing," "Shall We Gather at the River?").

The story of the phonograph turned out to be one of mechanical refinement and improvement. Electrical recording, which improved the sound vastly, came in the 1920's; the long-playing record in 1948; and since then the whole burgeoning industry of "high-fidelity" engineering, stimulated still more recently by the introduction of stereophonic

ENTERTAIN
"The Boys" with an
Edison Phonograph

Early phonographs (above, 1906) were steadily improved and enlarged as victrolas (below, 1914) for music at home and dancing out.

recording and playback and still quieter record surfaces. Between 1955 and 1962 the sales of phonograph records jumped from $80 million to $187 million. In 1963 over five million record players were sold. This opportunity to listen to good music well played and faithfully reproduced has been a great encouragement to musical good taste for many people.

Another source of pleasure which had moved into its amateur stages by 1900 was photography. It had been invented in 1837, but difficulties of manipulation and control had made it a hobby for specialists. The sequence had been as follows: first the daguerreotype, then the callotype, then the wet collodion plate (which had to be developed on the spot, and in darkness), then the dry plate, coated with sensitized gelatin. The whole process needed a genius to simplify it, and he came along in the person of George Eastman. During the eighties he developed a camera which was loaded with paper film at the factory—100 pictures— and was sold to the consumer with the famous instruction: "You push the button; we do the rest," which meant that the photographer sent camera and film together back to Rochester, where the film was developed and returned to him along with a freshly loaded camera. A little awkward, but the best that could be done. The original camera cost $25 and each roll of prints $10.

Then, with the invention of transparent celluloid film, Eastman standardized a process for sensitizing such film, and from 1891 on, the camera was "daylight loading" by the consumer himself. The speed of emulsions was still slow, and although it was possible for the photographer to set up a cumbersome powder-flashlight arrangement most pictures were taken out of doors, in the sunlight. The box camera gave way to one with a folding bellows; then came the 35-millimeter miniature camera. Home movie cameras

A Kodak Christmas

is the **Merriest Christmas**

Kodaks
$5.00 to $75.00

Brownie Cameras
$1.00 to $2.00

An ad for cameras in 1901

appeared on the market. Color was introduced in 1935. Lenses as well as films were improved, until today anyone who goes on a vacation or has a baby or a birthday or a new dog shoots rolls and rolls of film. And usually with pretty good success, so foolproof has the technique become. In 1959 retail stores sold over 400 million dollars' worth of cameras and photographic supplies.

There was a lot of do-it-yourself activity in the first years of the century. Some of it was hobby work, such as the making of bent iron objects, scroll cutting, and basketwork. Much of it, however, served practical purposes: wallpapering, furniture making, gardening, sewing and dressmaking. How-to-do-it books were on every publisher's list. You could learn "Taxidermy without a Teacher," "Rustic Carpentry," "How to Do Business," and even "Law and How to Keep Out of It." But it was only after World War II that do-it-yourself became really fashionable—partly, again, to save money in the face of mounting costs, but partly as a spare-time use of energy. Whole new industries sprang up to equip home workshops with all kinds of tools; the sale of portable electric tools grew from $6 million in 1946 to $95 million in 1953. It is estimated that over 11 million homes in the United States have home workshops, and that in 1963 American men spent $3,000,000,000 on do-it-yourself tools of all kinds.

Some 150 million rolls of wallpaper were sold to do-it-yourselfers in 1954. This represented 60 percent of the industry's total production, as compared with 28 percent ten years earlier. And as far as dressmaking was concerned, 100 million patterns were sold in 1963 (twice the rate of pre-war years); and some 136 million dollars' worth of sewing machines in 1961.

One point of all this is that *somebody* must be staying home evenings! As a matter of fact it is unrealistic to accept the stereotype that the modern home is something people flee from in search of more exciting entertainment elsewhere. Movies and spectator sports have combined, since 1900, to empty the house at times, but TV has brought sports and movies *into* the home and as a total influence has more than counterbalanced the exodus. A survey made in 1954 showed that an average of 23 percent of the adults who were interviewed devoted most of their leisure time to what were called "craftsmanlike activities." This compared with an average of 6.7 percent devoting most of their time to "commercial-type" activities—movies, spectator sports, etc.

The changing history of the theatre in the last sixty-odd years is both a record of shifting American tastes and a lessening contact with an institution that once had roots in every sizable town in the country. The twentieth century

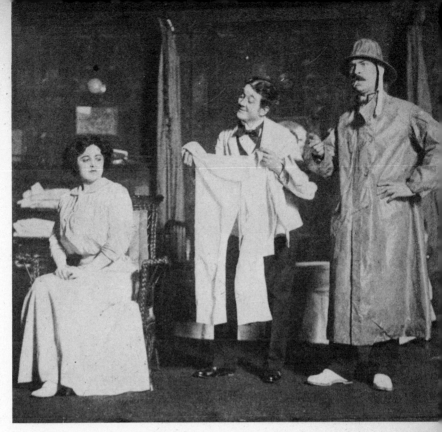

Maxine Elliot in a 1910 stage comedy, *The Inferior Sex*

saw the essential disappearance, except for outposts in the large cities and a centralization in New York City, of the professional theatre as an active force in cultural life. A larger percentage of Americans saw professional theatre in 1910 than in 1963.

Take vaudeville, for example. If not "cultural" it was for a long time at least vigorously American. Half a century ago the two-a-day flourished in some 2,000 small-time theatres across the land. By 1920 it was sharing theatre space with the ever-encroaching motion picture. By 1930 it was dead, and the hoofers, comedians, midgets, contortionists, and dog acts were history, except as they have been revived on Sunday-night television or have found asylum in night clubs. But vaudeville nourished some of the best comic talent in the history of American entertainment. Here are some of the names: Bustor Keaton, Al Jolson, W. C. Fields, Fanny Brice, Leon Errol, the Marx Brothers, Phil Silvers, Joe Cook, Ed Wynn, Fred Stone, Jimmy Durante, Weber and Fields, George M. Cohan. Even Ethel Barrymore and Sarah Bernhardt appeared at the Palace Theatre

Constance Collier in a 1910 drama, *Agnes, Duchess of Croucy*

in New York, the traditional heaven for vaudeville performers. Now it has all disappeared, along with the minstrel shows and the *Uncle Tom's Cabin* troupes.

In 1910 *Everybody's Magazine* lamented the decline of the theatre, citing the fact that 93 road companies had been disbanded the previous season. But there were still more than 300 such companies penetrating every corner of the provinces and playing one-night stands in Wichita, Ogden, Fargo, and Leadville, Colorado. Three years later the num-

Maude Adams as Peter Pan in 1905

ber had dropped from 300 to 200, and by the season of 1925 only 68 plays were on tour. Today, except in a few big cities, the "road" has been dead for some time. Although seasoned troupers like Katharine Cornell, Helen Hayes, and the Lunts (already an older generation) used to take plays on tour, frequently booking them into high school auditoriums and Masonic Halls, most regular theatres have long since been taken over by the movies.

Another outpost of the drama that has vanished is the old-fashioned stock or repertory company, composed of professional actors who set themselves up each season in the smaller cities (often in the local "opera house") and played a "new Broadway hit" each week, or sometimes twice a week. As late as 1929 there were over 200 repertory companies in the United States. A decade later there were only five; and today, except for the "summer theatres," they have disappeared, once again before the onslaught of increasing costs and the competition of the motion pictures and television.

How about the New York theatre? In the early century Broadway, as now, was the theatrical capital of the country, but it was a busier and lustier place. In 1927–28 (the peak year) 80 legitimate theatres housed 270 productions. Twenty years later there were 30 theatres and 87 productions. In 1961–62, only 56 productions. Moreover, throttled as producers are by snowballing costs, a good play which in the old days could be considered a success with only a modest run, today is a flop. As a result of this hit-or-flop economy some 75 to 80 percent of the shows produced are rated as failures. An investor has a better chance of getting his money back at the racetrack than from a Broadway play.

The reasons for the numerical decline of plays in the professional theatre are clear: its almost complete centralization in New York, the gigantic costs of production, and the increasing competition of other forms of entertainment. If you go to a movie every seat is a good seat and you don't have to pay up to eight dollars for a ticket that admits you to a drafty theatre built about 1920—a ticket which you had to get either through an expensive agency or by humble appeal to a supercilious box-office attendant. And if you don't feel like going to the movies, the monster in the living room will give you its own kind of dramatic fare at the turn of a switch. The wonder is that any plays open at all! But they do; the legitimate theatre has a sinewy resistance to extinction.

Around the turn of the century there were a lot of "escape" plays of the swashbuckling cloak-and-sword type, many of them adaptations of currently popular novels, from *If I Were King* (1901) to *The Prisoner of Zenda* (1908), which was to be re-created in a musical show half a century later. In 1900, William Gillette was appearing in *Sherlock Holmes* and the horses of *Ben Hur* were pounding nightly on the treadmill at the Broadway Theatre, with William S. Hart playing the part of the villain, Messala. For comedy you had the homespun humor of *David Harum*.

The quality of the serious drama of this period is illustrated by the career of Augustus Thomas, a typically facile dramatist whose plays were almost uniformly successful. For example, his play *The Witching Hour* (1907) deals with hypnotism and telepathy; indeed the crucial points of the play turn upon these effects, plus a welter of supercharged sentiment. The second act ends with Judge Prentice alone, holding a handkerchief that had belonged to his lost beloved and that still carries the scent of mignonette. A distant bell strikes two o'clock in the morning. "Margaret Price," mutters the judge, picking up her miniature. "People will say that she has been in her grave thirty years, but I'll swear her spirit was in this room tonight and directed a

Laurette Taylor and H. B. Warner in *Alias Jimmy Valentine* in 1910

decision of the Supreme Court of the United States." He puts the handkerchief to his lips and repeats: "The delicate odor of mignonette, the Ghost of a dead-and-gone bouquet." Curtain. One can only be glad that Broadway was not appointing justices to the Supreme Court!

Here, then, was a period in American drama up to about 1920, which liked to think of itself as realistic but which was either unabashedly sentimental or melodramatic or, when the situation asked for "strong" or serious treatment, served up its stories in the clichés of the theatre. The smell which lingers over these plays is the smell of theatrical greasepaint. At their best they had a kind of theatric gusto seen in the rapid colloquial comedy of George M. Cohan, the flag-waving Yankee Doodle boy who was the child of Broadway if ever there was one—actor, hoofer, songwriter, and playwright. He brought to a kind of contemporary perfection, and turned over to the next generation of comic writers the form of speech most American: the wisecrack.

It isn't often that the lines of artistic and intellectual change are indicated as clearly as they were in the American drama of the nineteen-twenties, when what is now called the "new" American drama sprang forth. In 1919 the Theatre Guild was established, and those who had sneered at the insurgents as "arty" and "experimental" had suddenly to reckon with a fresh and vital force in the theatre. The year 1920 saw also the production of Eugene O'Neill's *Beyond the Horizon* and *The Emperor Jones*. Just to repeat the names, in addition to O'Neill's, is to make clear the quality of the new movement: Sidney Howard, Maxwell Anderson, Elmer Rice, Robert Sherwood, George Kelly, Philip Barry, S. N. Behrman, George Kaufman, Marc Connelly. What the best playwrights of the twenties had in common was a desire to take a fresh look at contemporary life and to interpret it imaginatively and honestly. The pseudo realism of a generation earlier became a sincere realism involving a new appraisal of theme and character. It challenged the old conventions. It was Eugene O'Neill, of course, who cast the longest shadow over the serious modern theatre, not only in the twenties but on into the thirties and forties, and even posthumously into the fifties with such a play as *A Long Day's Journey into Night*.

American drama continued to follow the peaks and hollows of social and intellectual change. The thirties, and the Great Depression, were reflected in the theatre. A new school of socially conscious dramatists arose, angry at the inequities of modern life and writing propaganda plays on behalf of the underprivileged. Too often these were melodramatic stories punctuated by Marxist soapbox orations. But Clifford Odets, with his power of characterization and his exact ear for the cadences of American speech, combined art and social comment in such plays as *Awake and Sing* (1935) and *Golden Boy* (1938). The thirties saw the ripening, too, of some of the best talent that had appeared in the twenties. And Howard Lindsay and Russel Crouse wrote one of the most successful plays in the history of the American theatre: the warm and human comedy *Life with Father* (1935). The thirties also saw the production of two of the tenderest and most beautiful plays in American literature—Marc Connelly's superb recapturing of Negro folklore in *The Green Pastures* (1930), and Thornton Wilder's lovely and touching story of life in smalltown America, *Our Town* (1938). This latter is so simple and so true in its compassion and understanding that it rises to universals.

Arthur Miller and Tennessee Williams have been two of the most powerful talents in the more modern theatre, though Miller for a long period did not produce anything of significance. They reflect the temper of the second half of the century as fully as the older drama was conditioned by the moral and aesthetic confines of its time. In *Death of a Salesman* (1949) Miller treated with great dramatic effectiveness and eloquence, and with technical mastery, a theme only superficially indicated by the "salesman" framework. What he really dealt with were human hungers and aspirations, and the tragedy of loneliness and disillusion and failure. Failure in part because of the pressures of modern society but more deeply because of false ideals, spiritual limitations, and lack of self-knowledge.

Tennessee Williams represents a baffling combination of great talents and severe limitations. No one can write a dramatic scene more powerfully than he; no one can get a stronger sense of life into his characterizations. What disappoints one who wishes for a full dramatic statement by so skillful a playwright is his obsession with perversity and insanity, his steady dramatic involvement with twisted minds and distorted personalities. This obsession appears everywhere in his plays, compounded of sex (which he sees as the only important life urge), violence, and loss of contact with reality. One's complaint is not that this is not "real" or "true," or that it is merely unpleasant, for it is not the function of art to render comfortable pleasantries. The trouble is that such drama begins to withdraw as completely from the total spectrum of human reality as do the characters themselves. And these strictures apply with even more force to the later rise of the so-called "theatre of the absurd," which makes a religion of negation.

But however much one may wish for greater playwriting today it is clear that in our century the theatre has made vast strides in the direction of honesty and a desire to reach more deeply into the springs of human motive. At its best it is more mature and responsible, speaking more directly about more important themes than did the theatre of David Belasco's and Augustus Thomas's time.

There are reasons to hope, too, that live theatre may recapture at least part of the place it once held in American life. I have been speaking chiefly of the Broadway theatre. In the last ten or fifteen years one of the most encouraging signs has been the development of the "off-Broadway" theatre, which has produced very successfully at low cost in small auditoriums a wide range of excellent plays—from revivals of classic drama to the experimental work of exciting new dramatists. At their best these theatres have been financially as well as artistically successful. In a single week in 1964, one could have chosen to see any of twenty-eight musical or dramatic productions playing off-Broadway in New York City.

Equally encouraging has been the establishment across the country of new professional repertory theatres, from

One of the first movie films, *The Kiss*, lasted less than one minute.

New York to Minnesota to Texas to California. Nonprofessional and semiprofessional community theatres have also had a remarkable growth; and university theatres (many of them excellent) have taught audiences that there is a wide range of great plays which were not last year's Broadway hits. However ill the American theatre has seemed from time to time it has a remarkable tenacity for survival, even in the process of seeming to be overwhelmed by competing mass media of entertainment.

As live theatre disappeared as an experience for millions of people that loss was cushioned by the spectacular rise of another medium of entertainment: the motion picture.

When Edison developed his first Kinetoscope machine in 1894 he thought of it only as a toy and was not interested in the possibility of projecting pictures on a screen. The first "kinetoscope parlors" were merely peephole shows. Others, however, introduced the process of projection and when Edison's own "Vitascope" screen pictures were launched in 1896, a new industry was born. The first motion pictures did not tell a story; people were interested in anything that moved, whether horsecars, fire engines, pedestrians on Fifth Avenue, bathing beauties, parades. It is perhaps symbolic that one of the earliest commercial films was a close-up (comic) of an elaborately mustachioed gentleman kissing a coy lady. The film lasted a little less than a minute.

For some time, even after films began to tell a primitive

The Great Train Robbery in 1903 became a classic of early motion pictures.

Shooting a movie in 1910

story, they averaged only ten to twelve minutes. They were used in vaudeville houses as a device to clear the theatre between shows. But by 1903 Edwin S. Porter had produced *The Great Train Robbery*—an historical classic, because for the first time film told a connected story. In eight minutes you saw a theft, an escape on a railway train, a train holdup, a pursuing posse, and the ultimate killing of the bandits. Here were all the elements which were to become standard in the movie repertory: violence, the chase, retribution.

Even so, few people took the movies seriously in the early years. The first to promote the new invention were "quick buck" men who shot almost any kind of scene and rented the film to exhibitors or sold it, irrespective of content, for ten cents a foot. It was thought of as primarily entertainment for the lower classes and was praised, by those who philosophized about it, as "an effective protagonist of democracy," helping civilization to "permeate downward."

In 1905 an ingenious exhibitor rented an empty store

A favorite action scene in early movies

in Pittsburgh, Pennsylvania, put in 96 kitchen chairs, and charged five cents for admission. Thus was the first "nickelodeon" born. By 1907 there were some four or five thousand shabby picture theatres attended, it was estimated, by two million people daily, one-third of them children. Often the show, which was repeated eighteen to twenty times daily, was augmented by a ballad singer with colored slides, and before long the managers began to hire piano players to give proper atmospheric background to the stories on the "silver screen." This feature of tinkling musical accompaniment was to continue as long as the movies were silent. In 1907 the following pictures were advertised, among many others, each running about ten minutes: "Romay's Revenge (very dramatic)"; "Johnny's Run (comic kid chase)"; "Wizard's World (fantastic comedy)"; "Sailor's Return (highly dramatic)"; "Village Fire Brigade (big

175

Theda Bara as Cleopatra in 1917

laugh)"; "Ben Hur," done as a single reel; and "A Mother's Sin (beautiful, dramatic, and moral)." In 1910 there were 10,000 motion picture theatres in the United States, plus 1,400 theatres where movies were part of the program.

The acting in the early films was exaggerated, melodramatic. Characterization was rudimentary; the emphasis was on action. Prizefights were great popular successes, dating back to the Corbett-Fitzsimmons fight at Carson City, Nevada, in 1897. Actors were stage professionals who were "at liberty" or who didn't object to picking up a few dollars in their spare time. They could make as much as $25 a week. Manufacturing firms (they still weren't called "producers") would pay from $5 to $25 for stories "suitable for presentation."

As noted in one of the titles above, sin, as a dramatic

Ben Turpin

theme, entered the movie world early. It has continued as a
staple ever since, but in the early days when you met evil
you knew it was evil, and no mistake! Theda Bara (born
Theodosia Goodman, in Cincinnati) was the first of the
vamps, and within a three-year period this sultry siren made
some 40 pictures in which she destroyed men with her
"passion which was touched with death."

As the movies grew into a major industry they reflected,
and perhaps even helped influence, changing attitudes in
American life. In the twenties they were a part of the hard,
brazen, bathtub-gin-and-sex atmosphere which has remained
the stereotype of the decade. The innovation began in 1919

177

William S. Hart

with Cecil B. DeMille's version of James Barrie's quietly ironic English play *The Admirable Crichton*. It was retitled *Male and Female,* and the change was symptomatic. Soon Joan Crawford was dancing the Charleston in *Our Dancing Daughters*. Clara Bow became the "It" girl, and jazz-mad America, having abandoned its corsets, embarked (the movies would have you believe) on one vast spree. One film producer advertised: "Brilliant men, beautiful jazz babies, champagne baths, midnight revels, petting parties in the purple dawn." All this, plus a few Hollywood scandals, resulted finally in a sort of cleaning-up process and the submission by the industry to self-imposed moral codes which

Douglas Fairbanks Sr., Mary Pickford, Charlie Chaplin, and D. W.
Griffith

defined what movies could do and could not do—or at least
what they had to avoid *seeming* to do.

From the very beginning to the present day the Western
has been the form most notably successful, the one which
has shown the least change over the years. Any producer
could alter the basic formula only at his peril. It started
with William S. Hart, who was succeeded by other generations of cowboys, all hard-riding, fast-shooting men of honor
who created a sort of standardized crude epic, in which
gamblers and horse thieves, after furious battle, are always
vanquished in the final footage. Whether you saw it in a
nickelodeon in 1912 or in Roxy's Cathedral of the Motion
Picture in 1927 or at your neighborhood theatre in Techni-
color in the nineteen-sixties, or on your TV screen, the

179

Douglas Fairbanks Sr., Mary Pickford, and Charlie Chaplin having some off-screen fun.

theme and substance, though slicked up at times, have always been the same and will presumably always be popular.

In the twenties people in the larger cities jammed into huge movie palaces ornately overdecorated in the legend of Hollywood magnificence. And even in such a small city as Muncie, Indiana (35,000), nine picture houses were operating in 1923, from one to 11 P.M., every day.

In the thirties came a rash of gangster films (there were 50 such in 1931) which gave way to zombie horror films, which were supplanted by "science" horror films. Not until the sixties, however, did the Hollywood imagination produce the perfect combination of horror and sex: *A Werewolf in a Girls' Dormitory.*

Mack Sennett's hilarious Keystone Cops

Along with all this came, of course, a scattering of really distinguished films which helped us to realize that the motion picture could be an effective art form. But much of the sub-art was of the boy-meets-girl kind (no one would want to blacklist sex as a fact of life, ancient or modern), and the history of the movies is a parade of Great Lovers, from Valentino to John Barrymore to Greta Garbo to Elizabeth Taylor. The bread-and-butter of the industry lay in supercharged, romanticized sex—in general, a glamorized, fantasy world with very little resemblance to any known life. Yet the viewing of these productions was very much a part of everyday life. It was, to be sure, a declining part because of the rise of competing mass media. In 1945 the average weekly attendance in the theatres was 100 million, about what it had been in the late twenties; in 1950,

60 million. But even in 1958, when the industry was being decimated by television, 42 million people paid their way into movie theatres. And by 1964 business was on the upgrade again.

A survey such as this cannot begin to describe the multiple facets of a complex history—the early cliff-hanging serials; the wonderful world of early slapstick comedy, beginning with the Keystone Cops and culminating in the superb artistry of Chaplin (when did you last sit in a movie theatre and feel the waves of laughter rolling over you?); the cataclysm of the "talkies," when Al Jolson sang "Mammy" from the screen in 1927 and the industry underwent a major revolution. "You ain't heard nothing yet," said Jolson, and he was right. The rise of the multimillion-dollar "spectacular"—$2 million for the horse-race scene in *Ben Hur,* and $40 million to show on a wide screen that Antony loves Cleopatra; the production in recent years by independent producers of films which deal seriously with adult themes, though sometimes the word "adult" is used merely to identify stories of rape, prostitution, seduction, and cannibalism. The movies are a form of entertainment more thoroughly commercialized than anything Americans knew until the advent of TV, but they are capable at their best of great artistic accomplishment.

While movies were still in their infancy another medium of mass communication and entertainment was getting itself born. In 1899 some experimental apparatus which Marconi had established on an English lightship received an SOS signal from a helpless ship, and lives were saved. This was wireless telegraphy, not telephony, but in a few years the human voice was heard across miles of space, and soap opera was just ahead. Radio had to await, for practical purposes, the invention by Lee De Forest in 1907 of the audion tube to detect and amplify radio waves. In 1910,

"Daddy, let's get Los Angeles!"

Entertainment in the home, via radio, began in 1920. This is a 1924 ad.

De Forest broadcast, by radio from the Metropolitan Opera House, the voice of Caruso.

This new world of communication was first established commercially in the fall of 1920 when the Westinghouse Co. licensed Station KDKA, Pittsburgh. The first great broadcast, a milestone in radio history, was the Harding-Cox election report. By 1922 nearly 600 stations were in operation, and eager purchasers of primitive sets all over the country were sitting up until the early hours in order to be able to say at breakfast: "I got Salt Lake City last night!" As in the case of the early movie, the subject matter didn't make much difference; it was the excitement of being able to get anything!

Radio seemed relatively simple and relaxed in the early days, before it became institutionalized and commercialized. In 1921, 200,000 persons heard the on-the-scene report of the Dempsey-Carpentier fight in Jersey City. By 1922 the

The Mack Sennett bathing beauties

World Series was on the air. All sorts of sopranos and tenors flexed their voices before the microphones. Politicians began to make campaign speeches on radio, and comedians to wisecrack about the politicians. Soon some genius conceived the idea of sponsorship and advertising, and the guidelines of the new industry began to be drawn.

By 1930 there were 12 million sets in use; by 1938, 40 million. Networks were established. The Depression was on, and millions of people, unable to buy movie tickets even if free dishes were given away, gathered around the radio to listen to orchestras (perhaps Rudy Vallee's), popular song hits, drama, comedy. The great names in comedy were Eddie Cantor, Burns and Allen, Jimmy Durante, Ed Wynn, Edgar Bergen, Fred Allen, "Fibber McGee and Molly," and many others. The whole nation stopped talking at 7:00 P.M. every evening to tune in on "Amos 'n' Andy." A new form of radio drama was developed; people shivered with "The Inner Sanctum" mysteries or with Sherlock Holmes. Children's programs were developed more thrilling than anything out of Grimms' Fairy Tales: *Captain Midnight, The Green Hornet, The Lone Ranger,* and *Jack Armstrong, the All-American Boy.*

Soon the domestic dramas which came to be known as soap operas filled the airwaves. *Stella Dallas, Backstage Wife, Life Can Be Beautiful, Portia Faces Life,* and scores of others—scores literally, for as late as 1947 the networks sent out 25 of them a day. The characters in these dramatic gems lived in a world of catastrophe and hungry desperate love. Millions of women must have found these traumatic compendiums of fear and despair somehow satisfying. Certainly the programs did sell their sponsors' soap, or if not soap, toothpaste, mineral oil ("Relieves stomach acidity as well as *that other* condition!"), Postum, which was a complexion aid, it seemed, and Anacin, which even then was "made just like a doctor's prescription." James Thurber described the technique of soap opera when he said that it was "a kind of sandwich. . . . Between thick slices of advertising, spread 12 minutes of dialogue, add predicament, villainy, and female suffering in equal measure, throw in a dash of nobility, sprinkle with tears, season with organ music, cover with a rich announcer's sauce, and serve five times a week."

There was of course the news, which opened windows on new worlds, for it came from the loudspeakers with an immediacy the newspapers could never equal. "You were *there!*" In the thirties and during World War II people heard Hitler's rantings, Ed Murrow's broadcasts from London during the bombings, Elmer Davis's homely reassuring Midwestern voice giving news of the best or the worst; and above all Winston Churchill's bulldog messages to his nation in the gloomy days of 1940–41. The automobile shrank

Charlie Chaplin in *The Gold Rush,* 1925

space for Americans in the twentieth century, but it took radio to bring people within millionths of a second of each other.

No one was untouched by all this—and this is true, indeed, today, even though radio, with the coming of TV, seemed to go into a decline from which it might not recover. The United States had some 98 million radio sets in 1950, when TV was just getting started; it had 176 million in 1962. Yet the radio today serves a different purpose. FM (frequency modulation) radio has brought much distinguished music into the home, but AM (amplitude modulation) has become chiefly the refuge of local hucksters, and interrupts its commercials with the "forty hit tunes of the week." Jack Gould, the critic for *The New York Times,* describes it as "little more than a monotonous box spewing

Greta Garbo

forth musical trash, interminable commercials, and repetitious news-bulletins." At best it offers background music to listen to while one is doing something else—driving to work, shaving, or in the case of some young people, studying.

Television (which needs no long review here) was invented before World War II but did not come into its own until after the war. By 1950 there were 98 TV stations in the United States, and four million sets. In 1956, 35 million sets; and in 1962, 56.3 million. In 1962, 90 percent of our households had one TV set or more, and it has been estimated that during an average day some 100 million people listen to one or more programs—most of them to many more, if the surveys are accurate.

Paul Muni (center) in *Scarface*, 1932

Almost everything that has been said about popular taste and the movies applies to television—indeed, much of the daily fare is composed of old movies, and movie companies keep in business today by producing films for television. But because of its massive penetration into the American home, television has had an effect greatly exceeding that of any other mass medium of entertainment. Like the movies, it has had its fads and cycles—Westerns, situation comedies, hospital stories, crime stories. The density of the last has been disturbing to some guardians of public welfare. A few years ago the National Association for Better Radio and Television reported that during one week in Los Angeles the seven TV stations portrayed 223 killings of human beings. In addition there were 192 attempted murders, 83 robberies, 15 kidnappings, 7 attempted

W. C. Fields

lynchings, 6 dynamitings, and 11 extortions. More recently the trend has been to trade a few of these for "situation comedies," which if more banal are less lethal.

Here, however, as in the case of the movies, one must make clear that within the pattern of mediocrity many superior plays have been produced. And we have seen (perhaps under the stern eye of the Federal Communication Commission and its insistence upon "the public interest") a decent amount of very good news reporting of public events, to say nothing of some music concerts and discussion programs which are worth anyone's attention. It is true that all the pressures are toward mediocrity or worse. The industry is a confusing mixture of the F.C.C., the individual station, the networks, sponsors, advertising agencies, "packagers" who put together shows, the agencies who produce "ratings," and the individual consumer in his living room, who takes what is dished out and had better like it. But it is not clear that the public demands a much higher ratio of intelligent programming than it gets. Presented with the opportunity, one Sunday afternoon a few years ago, to watch *Wide, Wide World,* a program which dealt interestingly and factually with affairs of national or international importance, or to view an old film, *Rebecca of Sunnybrook Farm,* 90 percent of the audience elected the latter. The innocuous *Rebecca* would drive no one into crime, but it may be that most viewers need to search their own minds before they complain too loudly about the stupidities of television broadcasting.

To ask how people have amused themselves from 1900 on, then, is to discover the vast opportunities for mass entertainment which an almost incredibly accelerating technology has made possible. It is to see, at the same time, shifts and developments in American culture which have been reflected in the kinds of plays, movies, television they watch. It is also clear that there are certain continuities in American life which are just as important as the changes: that beneath the Arrow collar of 1909 there beat a heart which responded to the same stimuli as today. After all, *Rebecca of Sunnybrook Farm* hit the best-seller list in 1904, and Zane Grey's *The Riders of the Purple Sage* in 1912. Both sold well over a million copies.

7

Holidays and Sports

I<small>N</small> September, 1903, *The World's Work* printed an
article by Ralph D. Paine called "Are Riches De-
moralizing American Life?" In support of his thesis Mr.
Paine cited what he called "the sensational growth of luxury
in American life." For golf clubs and balls, he said, $2
million were sent annually, and for such sporting equipment
as that used in baseball, tennis, rowing, etc., $10 million.
The auto "will soon be ranked among the conveniences, if
not the necessities." He pointed out that in 1900, three
years after the introduction of what he called the "pastime,"
80 establishments in the United States were building cars
of 200 different types. In 1903, 7,000 autos were licensed
in the state of New York.

He went on to list the increases in luxury spending between 1890 and 1900 *beyond* the growth of the population:
millinery, 100 percent; jewelry, 35 percent; pianos, 40 percent; perfumery, 75 percent; sporting goods, 50 percent;
watches, 90 percent; silverware, 104 percent; malt liquors,
80 percent. No one was there to tell him that in 1962 about
$5,000,000,000, instead of $10 million, would be spent for
sports equipment of all kinds, or that there would be 9,000,-

191

000,000 registered vehicles in California in 1963. Mr. Paine did see clearly, however, that an industrial civilization was beginning to bring its benefits home to its citizenry and that people could accommodate themselves with remarkable facility to luxuries and recreations. But at this distance the turn-of-the-century concept of holidays and sports seems primitive and restricted. Neither had reached the stage of mass production we know today.

To begin with, people simply didn't have as much real income or as much leisure then as now. The average work-week was 60 hours instead of 40, and the idea of looking forward to a 35- or even 30-hour week would have seemed incredible. Paid vacations were unknown, except by the lucky few, whereas now they are enjoyed by some 95 percent of factory workers (up from less than 50 percent shortly after World War II), and nearly a quarter of those workers get three weeks off with pay each year. One forgets how recent this is; in 1953 there were six times as many people getting three-week vacations as in 1946. All this has of course helped to make possible the stupendous growth in leisure-time activities and expenditures.

Not that people didn't enjoy holidays, paid or unpaid, in the early century. Because travel was limited, most of the celebrations were local—picnics in the town park or out-side of town at the "trolley park," a device developed by the electric railways to encourage travel. Families enjoyed going to local baseball games, playing croquet or pitching horseshoes in the backyard, and sometimes attending the annual county fair or visiting circus. The Fourth of July, next to Christmas, was the big day of the year, crowded with games, parades, fireworks, band concerts, and patriotic speeches by local judges or politicians. When the century was still young, listening to full-blown holiday oratory which "made the eagle scream" was the delight of adults and the

"Having a good time" at the beach, 1905

duty of children. The Revolutionary War and our emancipation from England seemed much more recent than it did half a century later. And the Civil War, of course, was well within the memory of men and women still actively alive; as well as the more recent and much more romantic Spanish-American War.

The business folk who were financially better off took summer holidays at Newport, Bar Harbor, Tuxedo, Sara-

An elegant picnic on the beach, as painted by Harrison Fisher in 1906

toga, or even went to Europe. Those of more modest means sometimes attended regional Christian Endeavor Conferences, annual meetings of the State Baptist or Methodist Associations, or the reunion encampments of veterans of the Civil War. They could visit Put-In Bay or Chautauqua Lake, where the entertainment was edifying as well as recreational—staying in comfortable boardinghouses for a few dollars a week. For others the railroads ran multitudes of one- or two-day excursions, so that Philadelphians might visit New York, and New Yorkers could even visit Philadelphia. There were excursions to lakes, to the seashore, and above all to World's Fairs, which have always been a favorite American entertainment.

The World's Columbian Exposition, held at Chicago in 1893, was still a fragrant memory in the nineteen-hundreds. This "White City" was composed of Romanesque, Greek, and Renaissance architecture built of a kind of imitation marble. It has been said that it set back architecture in the United States for 30 years, but as a whole it brought vistas

Easter parade on the boardwalk at Atlantic City in 1905

Above, fireworks at the St. Louis Exposition in 1904. Below, the Panama-Pacific Exposition in San Francisco, 1915.

Golden Gate International Exposition, 1939–40

of a kind of global culture to over 27 million Americans. In 1901 came the Pan-American Exposition at Buffalo (where President McKinley was shot). In 1904 the St. Louis Centennial, with exhibits from 42 states and 53 countries. Nineteen million visitors saw 100 makes of automobiles on display as well as a wide variety of snake charmers and dancing girls. Other fairs followed: the Panama-Pacific Exposition at San Francisco in 1915; the Chicago Century of Progress Fair in 1933–34 (38.5 million people attended in the depths of the Depression); the Golden Gate International Exposition at San Francisco, 1939–40; and the

New York World's Fair in the same years. The most popular exhibits at all such fairs have always been the marvels of science and industry. Nowhere can one see more clearly or compactly our technological growth. Like other similar exhibitions, the New York World's Fair of 1964–65 was planned not only to display the wonders of the present but also to indicate the wave of the future. And such is our momentum that today presses always closer to tomorrow.

Many Americans were beginning to discover their own country in the first decades of the century. The magazines advertised low-budget trips to Colorado, the Rockies, California, and the Canadian Northwest. In 1897, 5,626 tourist tickets were sold to Colorado; in 1903, 65,126. It was estimated in 1905 that some 250,000 went to the Rockies for

New York World's Fair of 1939–40

California

is a land of sunshine,
more delightful in winter than
the Mediterranean.

There are ancient monastic ruins; picturesque types of Spanish and Indian life;
cultivated valleys of incredible fertility and loveliness, and mountains and meadows
ablaze with wild flowers in solid masses of gorgeous color.

The Santa Fe Route

An invitation to railway travel in 1900

their vacations. Rail rates often got down to $30 for the round trip from Chicago, and people could stay at a hotel or boardinghouse for from $5 to $40 a week. Really good accommodation, it was said, could be had for $9 a week.

The National Parks were still a new phenomenon. There were only four of them before 1900 (Mount Rainier, Sequoia, Yosemite, and Yellowstone), and magazines ran descriptive articles about them as they would have done for the Sudan. By 1904 there were 10 such parks with 121,000 visitors a year. In 1940, 7.5 million people visited the then 26 such parks; in 1963, 103 million people visited

Two ads of 1903, designed to catch vacationists

their 30 national parks, in addition to those who went to
national monuments. The national forests, too, have become
playgrounds for multiple millions of Americans. In 1963,
122 million people visited them for recreational use—pic-
nicking, fishing, hunting, riding, camping, swimming, skiing
—over six times as many as used them twenty years earlier
and three times as many as in 1953. The more civilization
we get the more people seemingly want to get away from it
and have the means and the time to do so. But the more
that people try to lose themselves the more difficult it becomes. Pessimistic observers predict the day when one will
be unable to throw a stone in a national forest without hit-
ting a Boy Scout or a hiker from Tuscaloosa. In July
or August even now you have to elbow your way around
the floor of Yosemite Park.

What has made all this possible, of course, are roads and automobiles and the collateral industries which have burgeoned in the effort to make life comfortable for the tourist, and to get part of his dollar. In 1900 the average traveler covered 500 miles a year, by horse and by rail. Today the average is 5,000 miles. In 1922 there were some 200 motels; today there are well over 60,000, doing a business of $1,500,000,000 a year. Tourism is Big Business, and vacations on the road the American Way of Life.

But if more people are seeing America, more also are visiting countries abroad. In his article in *The World's Work* Mr. Paine said that in 1902, 70,000 passengers (non-steerage) were carried to Europe from Atlantic ports. Few considered very seriously at that time travel in the Pacific or the Far East, though one early magazine steamship advertisement urged the delights of Tahiti! As far as Europe was concerned, it seemed to take less money than initiative to plan such a trip, for *The Overland Monthly,* in 1907, showed how the tourist could have a month's trip to England and Paris for a total cost of $250. It broke down this way: steamer fare (first class, round trip), $150; railroad fares, $25; hotels, $30; miscellaneous, $45. "Good Accommodations," the article ran, "can be reserved in all but the very finest hotels for $2 a day." You could get a six-week trip for about $300, and for two months you would need only $400. Who, it would seem, could afford to stay at home?

But easy junkets to Europe were still not a part of the American custom of vacations. Such trips began to become popular after World War I and the new discovery of Europe, and still more after World War II. In 1929, 517,000 United States citizens traveled overseas; in 1950, 676,000. In the next thirteen years travel tripled; in 1963, 2 million went abroad, four-fifths of them traveling by air. They spent over $3,000,000,000 overseas that year—the $45

Scenery at Yellowstone, and how to get there, 1902

"miscellaneous" in 1907, even adjusted to the modern dollars, would seem very small now.

Mobility, then, by wheel, ship, or air is taken for granted by the modern American. Frequently he travels not just on business or to see the sights but for some special holiday purpose. He climbs mountains, skis (on snow or water), skin dives, boats, fishes, hunts, or attends the World Series. And this brings us to the consideration of his absorption in sports—a big subject by itself, and no small part of his everyday life.

Like everything else, sports seemed much simpler in the early twentieth century. There were fewer of them and they received the devotion of a smaller fraternity; they had not yet widened into a national obsession. Newspapers which today take six pages to recount the previous day's happenings in sports got by very comfortably with one page in 1900. Not that Americans, within the limits of their time and money, have not always played. When one speaks of the modern organization of sports he should remember that swimming, fishing, and hunting have interested human beings long before Isaac Walton and Daniel Boone. (Indeed, there has been a return to a kind of simplicity in

202

Enjoying the Grand Canyon in 1905

sport which would have astonished Daniel Boone. A few years ago, in one season, the state of Michigan licensed 61,000 to hunt with bow and arrow!)

In the nineteen-hundreds children played simple games, for the most part around the house—marbles, tops, jacks, croquet, and often, at night under the sputtering arc light at the street corner, hide-and-go-seek. Baseball was endemic for the boys, but it was empty-lot baseball, with "scrub" teams. No one had heard of softball; they used cheaper versions of the regulation baseball, each one of which had to last until the stuffing was knocked out of it. It was all intensely interesting and very casual—no Little Leagues, no coaches, no uniforms, no high-powered organization. In the winter children skated on adjacent ponds; in summer they roller-skated up and down the flagstone sidewalks or swam in the nearest creek. No one offered them formal instruction or told them what games they had to play.

Their fathers went fishing when they could and hunted rabbits, squirrel, duck or deer as the occasion offered. Men and women played tennis together, sedately. Golf was looked on as a sport for the very well-heeled. Wrestling was something youngsters did in the backyard. Boxing (or rather "prizefighting") was for most people something to read about and in many cases to reprehend as brutal, repulsive, and more than faintly sinful. No heavyweight champion ever thought of lecturing on Shakespeare, as Gene Tunney did years later. In many states the sport was still illegal.

How a lady dressed for fishing in 1904

There was great interest in the high school football and basketball games, but as yet high school sports did not receive the local fanaticisms which later developed. Basketball was still very new. It had been introduced by Dr. James A. Naismith, its inventor, in 1892, and for some time was played chiefly in Y.M.C.A.s. As for horse racing, the sulky races at the county fair were as much as most people saw of this sport; few ever got near a professional track. The whole climate of betting associated with races outlawed them for big sections of Protestant America.

The story of spectator sports in the later twentieth century is one of fantastic expansion, the burgeoning of tennis, football, and golf from amateur to amateur-plus-professional status, with district, state, and national play-offs. Most American heroes in the twenties were sports heroes: Babe Ruth, Bill Tilden, Helen Wills, Jack Dempsey, Bobby Jones. In the case of boxing, wrestling, horse racing, and auto racing, the passing decades saw the creation of million-dollar gates for all kinds of spectator events. The Tunney-Dempsey fight at Chicago in 1927 took in over $2.5 million. Pari-mutuel turnovers at tracks grew to $55 million in 1940, and by 1963 had reached a total of almost $4,000,-000,000. The attendance at racetracks had sextupled in the same period. The total receipts from spectator sports grew from $30 million in 1921 to $274 million in 1960. Some 115 million watch basketball each year; 70 million, football. There is something both curiously modern and strangely quaint about an article in *Outing Magazine* for 1905 entitled: "Who is Responsible for Commercialism in College Sport?" Its conclusion: no professional coaches should be employed.

No one knows when it was first called "the national game," but no sport has its roots deeper in American life than baseball. There is still dispute about who invented it;

it is clear, however, that it got its start in the form we know it about the middle of the nineteenth century. By the time of the Civil War professional teams were touring the country. The National League was organized in 1876 and in 1900 the Western League changed its name to the American League. The first World Series was held in 1903 between the Boston Red Sox and the Pittsburgh Pirates; Boston won, five games to three. And by that time DeWolf Hopper was reciting at almost every performance of every play he appeared in across the country the poem which was on its way to becoming the national folk epic: "Casey at the Bat." "There was ease in Casey's manner as he stepped into his place." The verses had been written by a San Francisco newspaperman in 1888. Everyone knows the poem; few know that its author was Ernest L. Thayer.

Baseball grew steadily. The attendance in both major leagues in 1904 (the year Rube Waddell pitched for the Philadelphia Athletics and struck out 347 batters) was 5.5 million. By 1940 it was over 10 million and in 1963 nearly 21 million. This was only part of it, however. In addition to the major league teams were scores of minor leagues, from Class AAA down to D and E, all with their enthusiastic local followings. In 1903 there were 19 such leagues; by 1947 they had grown to 52 leagues, playing in 314 cities—a peak from which they later declined. Beyond all this are high school leagues, college leagues, municipal leagues, and what used to be called "twilight leagues," in which factories and businesses would field their teams. More recently the sport has seen the development of the Little Leagues, composed of youngsters who years ago would have been playing sandlot baseball but now have all the dignity of national organization, publicity, and their own World Series games. There are now nearly one million boys playing on 30,000 such teams. The statement of *Organ-*

Golfing near the rough in 1904

ized Baseball in the United States shows that in all leagues of all kinds there are 158,601 teams with 3,387,427 players. If you add to this the independent teams at the county and municipal level you get 200,000 teams with nearly 4.5 million players.

This is regulation baseball. Still more striking has been the growth of softball as a sport. In thousands of towns whole families go out to the park in the evenings to watch

Tennis, as reported in the social pages of 1903

their favorite teams play. Here too are sectional leagues with their tournaments, playing games watched each year by 125 million spectators—the largest total crowds of any spectator sport.

Next to eating apple pie, popcorn, and hot dogs there is no activity so uniquely and universally American as baseball. Like any traditional folkway, it has developed its own rituals: the seventh-inning stretch, the ingestion of cold drinks, the universal hostility toward the umpires ("kill the umpire!" was a cry in the 1880's). Legally, professional baseball has reached almost the position of a public utility. Few people stop to think that it is the kind of institution which newspapers called "the slave traffic" as far back as the late nineteenth century. Players can be shifted from team to team at the will of the owners and are bought and sold like any piece of horseflesh. As long as a player chooses to make his living by the game, he has no control over where, in what conditions, or under whose management he plays.

Baseball is not merely a sport; it is also an influence on American speech. Consider how many idioms, puzzling to foreigners, come directly from the game. "He's off his base"; "he's a foul ball"; "he has two strikes against him"; "he'd better keep his eye on the ball"; "he went to bat" for his friend; he "pinch-hit" for his colleague. Put these together with such sayings as "The Secretary of State carried the ball while the President was quarterbacking the government," or "With a forward pass from the governor he made an end run around the Securities Exchange Commission" and you have a national way of life in which sports get fused (or confused) with public policy.

Many people are involved in the playing of spectator sports, but the astounding growth within the twentieth century has been that of "activity" sports, engaged in by the average citizen as a purely individual exercise. Here is the great democratization of recreation.

Take golf, for example. Of respectably ancient lineage it was nevertheless considered an upper-class activity in 1900, and in 1902 there were only 1,122 golf courses in the country. Theodore Roosevelt warned President-elect Taft against playing a game associated with "dudes" and "snobs." But by 1962 there were 7,070 courses. More important are the number of people playing these courses, of which some 1,000 are public links. The National Golf Foundation estimates that 5.5 million people play golf today, up 45 percent from 1957. It is a sport which the truck driver or the hairdresser plays just as enthusiastically and perhaps more expertly than the millionaire of yesterday. Many of the best courses in the country are maintained by industries for their employees.

The history of bowling is just the reverse of this. The bowling alley of the early century was distinctly a place of lower-class entertainment, frowned upon by most stable citizens as just next door to the saloon—which it often was. Today the business executive takes his whole family into an airy, well-lighted, comfortably furnished building for an evening's bowling. The surroundings are as respectable as a high school gymnasium but more comfortable, complete with all services, from soft drinks and candy bars to baby-sitters. Your executive bowls; that is, if he can get in, for most nights of the week the alleys are crowded with more than a million teams which play on regular schedules. In 1961–62, 28 million bowlers rolled balls in the more than

This was aquaplaning in 1914.

130,000 lanes across the country—exactly some 22 times as many lanes as existed in 1924.

Of outdoor sports, hunting and fishing have always been the most popular with American men, fishing particularly. It was estimated that more than 25 million people went fishing in 1960. I said "men," but more than a third of this number were women. Many others went water-skiing or skin diving; it is said that some 5 million people put on flippers and search the underwater world today. Five million others ski in winter.

Boating, particularly, outboard-motorboating, has shown in recent years the most astounding increase of all sports, the more amazing because it involves a considerable investment. The number of outboard-inboard motors in use more than tripled between 1952 and 1959. Some 6.5 million were in use in 1963, in which year Americans spent $2.5 million on boats of all kinds. Boat trailers ride the highways, and the traffic on hundreds of inland lakes and waterways approaches weekend holiday saturation. Seventy-five-horsepower outboards churn the waters, driven, frequently, by people who had never been in a boat until they picked one off the floor at the last motorboat show, and who aren't exactly sure what a right-of-way is. One native Kansan has been reported as saying: "Come Sunday, you won't be able to stir 'em with a stick!"

In 1902 Americans spent $12 million for sports equipment. Today it is a multimillion-dollar business and has stimulated many subsidiary industries, not the least of which is the making of "sport clothes" for women, some of which are actually worn in the playing of sports. They cover less of the woman than in 1900 but cost a lot more. From beaches to national parks, from ski lifts to bowling alleys, from baseball diamonds to mountain climbing, America lives a happy share of its life in the context of sports and holidays. Sometimes their demand upon the individual seems almost compulsive, but no one has argued that fresh air and exercise are not good for people or that the democratization of recreation—fewer big yachts and more outboard motors, less polo and more camping-out—is not a net gain for most Americans.

8

The People Laugh

O<small>NE</small> of the most engaging qualities of human beings is their ability to laugh. To know *why*
people laugh has puzzled philosophers and critics, and
nothing is duller than an attempt to analyze humor. James
Thurber described at least his own brand accurately when
he said that "humor is a kind of emotional chaos told about
calmly and quietly in retrospect." But as E. B. White (no
mean humorist himself) once put it: "Humor can be dis-
sected, as a frog can, but the thing dies in the process, and
the innards are discouraging to any but the pure scientific
mind. Humor has a certain fragility, or evasiveness, which
one had best respect. Essentially, it's a complete mystery."

Certainly no simple explanation will serve. It ranges
from the practical joke and the custard pie to cynical pessi-
mism; from the pun to the humorous evaluation of some
of the deepest things in life. It includes the gag, the anecdote, the epigram, tall stories, parodies and burlesques, the
extended sketch, the drama, the novel. It extends from
nonsense—pure zaniness—to criticism: literary, political,
social. It can sometimes make even the horrible and the
grotesque seem comic—witness Charles Addams's cartoons.

And such are its vagaries that what seems excruciatingly funny to one person is just pointless to another. There is one safe rule to follow: never tell your friend that he lacks a sense of humor. You may tell him he's surly, egotistical, penurious, ugly, that you suspect he beats his wife or that he is politically unsound—but never that he doesn't know what to laugh at.

The basic jokes were the same in Aristophanes' time, presumably, as now—mothers-in-law, host-and-guests, taxes, children, politicians, stinginess, pomposity, he-and-she. But fashions in humor change and the methods and techniques of the humorist vary from generation to generation. You can learn a good deal about the social climate of a given period if you discover what seemed funny to its people.

Early American humor was a frontier humor—Yankee (generally meaning New England) humor, Hoosier (Midwest, especially Indiana) humor, backwoods humor—leaning heavily on strong exaggeration. It showed up in tall stories; a whole folklore was built on the superhuman achievements of Paul Bunyan, Davy Crockett, and Mike Fink. Later on it relied just as heavily on misspellings, and we got Artemus Ward, Petroleum V. Naseby, Josh Billings, and later Finley Peter Dunne, whose Mr. Dooley spoke Irish brogue. Mr. Dooley was a genuine creation. If most of this kind of humor seems forced and farfetched to us today it is because the trick of misspelling is a purely conventional one. To spell "half" as "haf," "comes" as "kums," and "to" as "tu" doesn't really add much to the joke; it repels us, rather. But much of what Mr. Dooley has to say in dialect is as witty and penetrating as any modern humorist could strive for.

On capital and labor:

"Capital still pats Labor in th' back, but only with an axe. Labor rayfuses to be threated as a frind. It wants

214

to be threated as an inimy. It thinks it gets more that way. . . ."

"They ought to get together," said Mr. Hennessy.

"How cud they get anny closer together thin their prisint clinch?" asked Mr. Dooley. "They're so close togither now that those that are between them are crushed to death."

On the Vice-Presidency:

"It is princap'lly, Hinissy, because iv th' vice-prisident that most iv our prisidents have enjoyed such rugged health. Th' vice-prisident guards the prisident, an' th' prisident, afther sizin' up th' vice-prisident, concludes that it wud be better for th' counthry if he shud live yet awhile."

On Democrats:

"Man an' boy I've seen th' dimmycratic party hangin' to th' ropes a score iv times. . . . I've gone to sleep nights wondhrin' where I'd throw away me vote afther this an' when I woke up there was that crazy-headed ol' loon iv a party with its hair sthreamin' in its eyes, an axe in its hand, chasin' raypublicans into th' tall grass."

On Republicans:

"Histhry always vindicates th' dimmycrats, but niver in their lifetime. They see th' thruth first, but th' trouble is that nawthin' is iver officially thrue till a raypublican sees it."

This kind of cracker-box-philosopher humor, immensely popular at the beginning of the century, has always had a grass-roots hold on the American people. For many years they followed in newspapers the daily appearance of a fence-sitting yokel, "Abe Martin," who tossed out such pithy comments as "Bein' poor ain't no disgrace, but it might as well

215

Humor in *Life*, 1915: "Oh, George, you've broken your promise." "Never mind, dearie. I'll make you another."

be!" Or his small-town news item, which says more about changing times than it seems to: "Druggist Lem Small severed an artery while fillin' a prescription for a pork sandwich." George Ade, with his *Fables in Slang,* was an offshoot of this school of vernacular humor, which frequently made a social comment as well as a humorous point.

Another reason some of the humor of half a century or more ago seems flat is that it relied on an elaborate verbal and pictorial embroidery to surround a small joke. A slight story would be rhetorically expanded in a full treatment until the humor toppled under the weight of its superstructure. The old humorous magazines such as *Life* and *Judge* and *Puck* were filled with routine he-she jokes which took paragraphs to tell. The typical cartoon, like the pictures in the old *Punch,* did not pretend to be funny in itself, but served merely as an illustration for the joke printed beneath, and could just as well have been detached from it—if even then you had wanted to read what the vicar said to the milkmaid when the pig got under the fence, and what the milkmaid said to the vicar, and how the vicar replied. Beautifully drawn full-page pictures would accompany sedate jokes without any real edge or point—at best whimsical; at worst, banal. *Life* in 1915 ran "cute" dog pictures or sweet views of little girls embroidering wall mottoes. *Harper's* in

"Mama, can a fellow have ice cream every day in Heaven?" "My dear, you wouldn't want it there." "I always knew Heaven wasn't the place it's cracked up to be." (*Life*, 1901)

1907 could descend to illustrated puns: "Do you know, he puts me in mind of an ocean liner." "Why?" "Because he is always toed in."

As the horse-and-buggy days disappeared into the nineteen-twenties they were still remembered in the cartoons of such humorists as Clare Briggs and H. T. Webster, who were guardians of a tradition established a little earlier by

Life covers in 1901, left, and 1927, right

Sentiment in *Life* in 1915

John McCutcheon. Briggs' cartoons *Mr. and Mrs.*, *Ain't It a Grand and Glorious Feeling?*, *When a Feller Needs a Friend*, and Webster's series on *The Timid Soul* and *The Thrill That Comes Once in a Lifetime* depicted memories of boyhood and a rustic or small-town world. It was gentle humor, kindly and sympathetic, nostalgic and a little wistful, reflecting an America and a countryside that had disappeared or was fast disappearing.

With the onslaught of the twenties, however, humor took a brisker, brassier turn, and John Held, Jr., became the cartoonist-commentator for the age of jazz babies and the school of college humor and flapperdom. *Life* ran jokes and pictures which would have outraged its readers a decade or two earlier. But it was the establishment of *The New Yorker* in 1925 which marked the watershed of American humor. As it blossomed, the old *Judge* and *Life* declined and finally disappeared. Under the editorship of Harold Ross *The New Yorker* assembled a stable of brilliant cartoonists: Peter Arno, Helen Hokinson, George Price, William Steig, Sidney Hoff, Whitney Darrow, Jr., and others. Readers saw the emergence of a new type of cartoon—captionless, or with a one-line caption where the picture and text are integrally related, and the one doesn't make sense—or humor—without the other. One remembers such classics as the Charles Addams sketch of the ski tracks going downhill, separating as they reach a tree and then coming to-

gether on the other side; no words needed, or possible! Or the George Price picture of the man frantically disentangling the ivy which is wrapped around his house, and his wife's shouted warning: "Look out, George, here it comes again!" Or the picture by Whitney Darrow, Jr., showing the mattress salesman in the store, asleep on a bed, while the woman customer tells a worried floorwalker: "He was explaining about the inner springs, and just dozed off." These perfect marriages of pictures and captions, like so much of the best humor, induce quiet laughter. Sometimes these cartoons were satirical, sometimes just madcap, rooted in fantastic situations but beautifully planned in terms of the sudden or unexpected.

The New Yorker became labeled as a magazine of sophis-

Left, one of the many *When a Feller Needs a Friend* cartoons by Clare Briggs, 1929. Above, a John Held Jr. illustration in *Life*, 1927.

ticated metropolitan humor. In its early stages it cultivated this image; it was not written, it declared, "for the old lady from Dubuque." As a matter of fact it has never been "sophisticated" in the derogatory sense, and it is read avidly by Dubuque. It established a tradition of witty urbanity and healthy irreverence, but much of its wit has been directed *against*, is pentrating kidding of, pseudo sophistication. When it has grown serious, as it has sometimes, its anger has been against the illiberalisms and the social and international indecencies of modern times.

The humorous writers whom Ross gathered around him in the late twenties were a constellation unique in the history of American humor, and as long as they continued to write, through the thirties and forties, humor in this country enjoyed a kind of Golden Age. The writers were people like E. B. White, Robert Benchley, Frank Sullivan, Dorothy Parker, Ogden Nash, Woolcott Gibbs, James Thurber, and S. J. Perelman.

Different as they were, most of these people had certain qualities in common. Perelman dealt much with parody, and achieved great humorous effects by applying careful logical analysis to completely illogical situations. Benchley too was at his best in his burlesques—a sort of deadpan humor. But more significantly, Perelman in his *The Road to Miltown, or, Under the Spreading Atrophy;* Thurber in *My World and Welcome to It;* Benchley in *My Ten Years in a Quandary* and *Benchley Beside Himself;* Sullivan in *A Pearl in Every Oyster*—all these made great comic capital out of their authors' frustrations and limitations. They battle their phobias; they lie on what Thurber called the "bed of neuroses." The details of life, as they describe them, seem to win all the battles. They have trouble with overcoats, with imperfect vision, with telephones, stepladders, shoelaces, door keys, overshoes, plumbing and automobiles. They are hypochrondriacs; they quake at loud noises, open places, closed places, high places. They are perplexed and baffled —Thurber, in both his cartoons and his stories, by predatory women or cocktail party banalities or even just leaking electricity. Benchley's famous "Treasurer's Report" is a study in frustration, induced by his attempt to grapple with financial statements which he can meet only with an elaborate air of nonchalance.

Pain and embarrassment are often the staple of these humorists. As White says, "They have always made trouble pay. . . . Beneath the sparkling surface of these comical dilemmas flows the strong tide of human woe." Thurber described the occupational neuroses of the humorist well in his preface to *My Life and Hard Times:* "The little wheels of their invention are set in motion by the damp hand of melancholy. Such a writer moves about restlessly wherever he goes, ready to get the hell out at the drop of a pie-pan or the lift of a skirt." It may be that this gives the reader the sense of superiority which some critics claim is at the heart of all humor. *We* don't let shoelaces or stepladders baffle *us!* Children don't get *us* down, and humorous writers are always being exasperated by their own or others' children—others', usually. Ogden Nash put it succinctly in his poem "To a Small Boy Standing on My Shoes while I Am Wearing them":

> The interest I take in my neighbor's nursery
> Would have to grow, to be even cursory.

We're above this, and *yet*—we all realize that inanimate objects, as well as people, have at times baffled us. There is a sense here of recognition of common human experience which comes home to us. It is at least within the realm of our possible experience, and reaches us with an uncomfortable sense of truth as well as of comedy. The best humor does make you think; it is one kind of evaluation of life. As White says: "It plays, like an active child, close to the big hot fire which is Truth. And sometimes the reader feels the heat."

This is true in such a hilarious anecdote as Thurber's "The Night the Bed Fell," where a household of eccentrics suffer an extended midnight cataclysm that is excruciatingly funny. And at the other end of the spectrum it emerges mildly in the understatement of the story about the man who ordered a plate of soup in a restaurant. The headwaiter asked him how he liked it. "Well," he replied wistfully, "I'm kind o' sorry I stirred it."

In any event, the period between the World Wars saw the production of a quantity and quality of humor which was fine beyond all question. Some of the best of it was satiric, a development which deserves some special attention, for the nature of satire in any period tells us much about the social climate of the time.

Satire is an oblique way of commenting on the foibles, pretensions, and imperfections of human nature. It can run the whole range from concealed savagery and bitterness through sarcasm and ridicule to burlesque and parody, and finally to a gentler kind of ironic recognition of the gap between what we like to think we are and what we really are. There is no better way to ventilate absurdity or to let the stuffing out of a stuffed shirt.

James Thurber once said that we are a nation of slapstick people. "We invented the gag," he wrote, "the bellylaugh, and the hotfoot. We are not a nation that chuckles." If this is true, Mr. Thurber must have been a little puzzled by his own vast popularity. But the comment is more nearly true of American humor around the turn of the century. About the only satirist then whom one could take seriously (this is not paradoxical!) was Finley Peter Dunne. His Mr. Dooley, whom we have seen earlier, poked fun at all kinds of sacred cows: politics, education, golf—particularly politicians. His later counterpart in the twenties was Will Rogers, who needled kings and presidents but whose punches were delivered with such an amiable smile that they didn't really hurt.

The twenties and thirties saw a sudden welling-up of first-class satire. Here were Sinclair Lewis in the novel, and a little later, J. P. Marquand; George S. Kaufman and Marc Connelly and George Kelly in the drama; in radio, Fred Allen and Henry Morgan; and in the magazines Corey Ford, Donald Ogden Stewart, Ring Lardner and the others mentioned earlier, from Benchley to Sullivan to Gibbs and Thurber. All of these were writing at the same time, and American complacency was never safe while they were operating.

Kaufman in *Beggar on Horseback* (1924) and *Of Thee I Sing* (1931) satirized politics, and the stupidities of business and material success; as did Lewis in *Main Street* (1920) and *Babbitt* (1922). Some of the satire reached into crevices of arrogance and prejudice, as in the Thurber-Nugent play *The Male Animal* (1940), partly a comedy about ex-football heroes who never grow up but at its heart an attack on those who would limit freedom of speech. The most savage of the satirists in the twenties was Ring Lardner, who rose to popularity as a writer of comic stories about dumb baseball players. It wasn't until the critics "discovered" him that he was seen to be a major satirist, angry about cruelty and arrogance and acquisitive materialism and cheap vulgarity. At bottom he was melancholy about the so-called civilization he saw around him. Read his "Love Nest" and his "Champion" if you can take your satire straight.

This broad stream of satire was strong in the thirties, when one might have expected it to dry up under the hot winds of the Depression. E. B. White was one of the great ones here, and one of the fine writers of our time. He is a satirist but more than satirist. He has written everything from ironic verse to stories to essays to fantasy. Even in his fantasy he is reflecting thoughtfully and quietly about the strange anachronisms and improbabilities of our time, and putting in a persuasive plea for generosity and compassion. White not only says witty things freshly, he says wise things well. Similarly, Thurber wrote with sympathy, not contempt, for the human race. But the other side of this was an unerring instinct to probe bigotry and stupidity, and the fads and follies which are a part of our human heritage and cannot be labeled as the property of a particular age.

In the late forties and throughout the fifties satire pretty well ceased to be a part of one's everyday experience. It became immobilized in a kind of creeping paralysis. Some of the aging giants like Thurber and Perelman were still around, but Henry Morgan lost his sponsors and Fred Allen died sad and embittered about the hard days upon which satire had fallen. Al Capp, who once wrote social satire into his comic strip, confessed that he had to reform. "For the first fourteen years [of the strip]," he said, "I reveled in the freedom to laugh at America. But now America has changed. The humorist feels the change more, perhaps, than any one. Now

Eddie Cantor

there are things about America we can't kid." Corey Ford, in 1958, said: "We're afraid to laugh." "The most dangerous thing about writing today," said Thurber in 1957, "is that Americans are afraid to laugh about their own institutions." These people believed that a healthy society can afford to laugh at itself.

This fear to criticize reaches a kind of ultimate when one comedian has to get permission from another comedian before he can burlesque him (a legal fact!). It is seen in other ways, too. No more telling jokes about national minorities; the blackface comedian of the twenties is unthinkable now. No more Negro jokes or Jewish jokes or German jokes or Irish jokes. This may well be a healthy symptom of social progress, an increasing sensitiveness toward the dignity of minorities. "Old Black Joe" just doesn't seem appropriate today. But it also reaches extremes so acute as to be almost morbid, betraying not really social strength but social uncertainty and insecurity.

As far as magazines were concerned, James Beatty, Jr., told a story of a cartoon in the fifties showing "a pathetic gentleman at the optometrist's. He came to be fitted for glasses. He says, 'I'd like to see a little less clearly, please!' This has been rejected at least twice, not because it isn't funny, but because it's pessimistic!"

Perhaps as a kind of escape from a social climate that would not tolerate satire—an escape into something more savage, and meaningless—the fifties saw the rise and happily the decline of a thing known as "sick" humor. The type joke was: "But aside from that, Mrs. Lincoln, how did you enjoy the play?" This "humorous" form descended into sub-basements much lower than that. It reflected, perhaps, a sick age; it was not humor, but an attempt to shock—a revolt by the emotionally adolescent and the pseudo intelligentsia against they knew not what. In the process it debased human nature; to the extent that it was popular it was clinical evidence of a group neurosis.

The decline of satire was seen by some as tied in with the decline of humor in general, at least as it appears in the mass media, and has been traced partly to the fact that TV, for instance, sucks comedians into its insatiable jaws and then disgorges them when the gag writers can't any longer keep up. It is called overexposure and is implicit in the nature of the medium; there simply aren't that many good comedians or comic writers in the world. It burned out Sid Caesar and George Gobel and Art Carney and many lesser lights. It would have burned out Will Rogers and W. C. Fields if they had lived to see it and had submitted to it.

The mention of these last names is a reminder that so far we have been considering chiefly *written* humor, whereas some of the lustiest humor has always been found in the "act" rather than the written word. However broad much of it was, a good deal of the comic tradition in America stems from the old days of vaudeville. When Ziegfeld was

W. C. Fields

Will Rogers

glorifying the American girl in the *Follies* he was also creating a showcase for some of our best comic talent—Will Rogers, W. C. Fields, Eddie Cantor, Al Jolson, Ed Wynn, among others. And at the same time, in the wonderful world of Mack Sennett and Hal Roach, movies were convulsing audiences all over the nation: the Sennett cops, Mabel Normand, Chester Conklin, Buster Keaton, Laurel and Hardy, and Ben Turpin. This was the time also of Charlie Chaplin and Harold Lloyd. Here the comedy was visual rather than verbal, but the beautifully timed sight-gags of this comic universe were very funny indeed. Custard pies are now back in fashion; the interesting thing is how heartily people laugh when they see those movies revived!

There is evidence that satire may be emerging from the storm cellar. It has kept a thin but steady line of advance in such cartoonists as Bill Mauldin, Walt Kelly, Jules Feiffer.

It has been revived noticeably in Mort Sahl ("the egg-heads' comedian"), in the fine scenes of social desperation of Mike Nichols and Elaine May, in Shelley Berman and Bob Newhart (all of whom, however, tend to wear themselves out repetitiously). It appears in the skits of such groups as the Second City Players, who have the courage of their own sanative irreverence. It is strange, however, that the early sixties learned that satire could still be played, and enjoyed, from visiting groups of Englishmen who appeared on our shores. Here, suddenly, were such evenings in the theatre as those offered by Flanders and Swann in *At the Drop of a Hat;* by the sharply incisive *Beyond the Fringe* group, and by *The Establishment.* Some of the best satire of these visiting writer-players dealt with British personalities and institutions and therefore could be laughed at by Americans without guilt feelings. But much of it attacked hypocrisy, racial prejudice, and the general bumbling affectations and inconsistencies of human beings. Perhaps Americans are moving into an atmosphere of intellectual liberation in which satire can be what it should be, a corrective for the clichés and conformities of life and a cool appraiser of some of our own social and political deficiencies.

There remains one kind of humor which over the years has been closer than any other, perhaps, to the daily lives of most Americans. It is estimated that 100 million people read the comic strips each day in the newspapers, more than read any other section of the paper, including the sports pages. Comic books are merchandised by the uncounted millions. And a little collection of *Peanut* sketches in the form of a very small volume called *Happiness Is a Warm Puppy* sold well over 200,000 copies at two dollars apiece, shortly after publication. Here is humor at its peak

Peanuts, above, is one of the most popular comic strips of today. Below, *The Yellow Kid*, 1897, was the first comic strip.

Three early and famous cartoon strips were, above, *Happy Hooligan*, 1930; facing page, top, *The Katzenjammer Kids*, 1904, and bottom, *Buster Brown*, 1905.

level of acceptance. How did it begin and what is it now?

Richard Outcault's *The Yellow Kid*, a raucous uninhibited character in a back-alley setting, appeared in 1895 and is identified as the first comic strip. The next year saw the appearance of Opper's *Happy Hooligan* and Dirks' *The Katzenjammer Kids*. Soon *Buster Brown* and *Foxy Grandpa* were delighting youngsters. In 1909 Bud Fisher drew his first *Mutt and Jeff*, and in 1912 George McManus launched *Bringing Up Father*—his Maggie and Jiggs becoming enduring classics of the cartoon world. It was a strange world, this of the early comics, and still is, for many of the characters seem to go on forever. It was the "Thap! Whap! Bang! Crash! Zowie! !$**!*" school of hard knocks, dealing for the most part with shady characters who met momentary disaster each day in the final frame. Happy Hooligan was always being defeated or humiliated by his sadistic acquaintances; Jeff usually landed on his rear after a wallop from Mutt (who spent most of his time at the race-

Three comic strips still widely read today are *Bringing Up Father*, top of opposite page; *Gasoline Alley*, bottom of opposite page, and *Mutt and Jeff*, above.

track); the Katzenjammer Kids were ingenious young fiends who perpetrated a continuous series of indignities against the Captain. Jiggs, an Irish laborer grown rich but still addicted to corned beef and cabbage, made a career of escaping Maggie's clutches to run down to the corner saloon. It was a lusty, primitive, and violently slapstick world. Each strip told a separate anecdote daily.

As time went on and the comics came to be syndicated widely, some of the strips started to tell a continued story, and a kind of sophistication crept into the drawings if not into the narrative conception. Tarzan began his jungle adventures and all kinds of adventure strips sprang to life—*Superman, Flash Gordon, Dick Tracy;* plus the later excellent draftsmanship of Caniff's *Steve Canyon.* Along with these were the domestic dramas of *Little Orphan Annie* and *Gasoline Alley,* the best representatives of a school which was sentimental and touching—seldom comic—but which became, as someone said, "a factor in shaping a nation's emotional and intellectual responses." At their worst the uncomic strips were the agonizing pictorial equivalent of the soap operas which were flooding the airwaves. Taking the "comics" as a whole, the word today is a courtesy title which doesn't even begin to describe most of them.

If the intellectual responses of the nation were to be equated with some of the domestic strips, they gave a strange reflection of American home life. Father was always a boob, victimized and tyrannized over by his shrewder wife and his insolent and rapacious children. Ultimately, however, other strips were created which have become the aristocracy of the "funnies," whose stories are told with humor and subtlety. They have a good amount of penetration into human nature and, through a kind of satirical mythology, into the social structure of American life. Here are Al Capp's *Li'l Abner,* Walt Kelly's *Pogo,* and Charles Schulz's *Peanuts,* the latter a warm and sympathetic account of the world of children, followed enthusiastically by adults who suffer with Charlie Brown and his inferiorities and are appalled by the termagant womanhood of the domineering Lucy.

Just as jazz became eventually a highbrow cult, the comic strip also has been taken under the wing of serious intellectuals. Gilbert Seldes in his *Seven Lively Arts,* as early as 1924, called *Krazy Kat* high art. More recently books have been published analyzing the comics from every conceivable cultural point of view. Sociologists, anthropologists, psychologists, and psychiatrists have brought their disciplines to bear upon the implications of Dick Tracy and Superman. The latter has been called a "father figure," Charlie Brown "an inner-directed person in an outer-directed society." It has been suggested that Little Orphan Annie "appeals to those who feel weak or frustrated," that the strip offers "hate objects." *Gasoline Alley* "permits the readers to identify directly with the leading characters in their adventures"; *Dick Tracy* "satisfies sadistic or aggressive impulses." The names of James Joyce and Sigmund Freud have been invoked to interpret *Pogo*. Al Capp's symbolism in *Li'l Abner* has been compared with that of T. S. Eliot. None of these scholars means to be funny, but it is well, perhaps, that most readers don't encounter their dissertations, only continue to enjoy the comics—presumably all 200 of them listed in *Editor and Publisher*.

The comics still show the continuities as well as the changes of American taste. Jiggs and *Mutt and Jeff* and the *Katzenjammer Kids* are still read by new generations of readers. *Superman* and *Flash Gordon* in the sixties are only an atomic-age extension of *Little Nemo* of 1906.

Indeed American humor as a whole, with its currents and eddies, its retreats and its advances, its grotesqueries and its subtleties, testifies to the remarkable endurance of the will to laugh. At its most typical it is an affectionate, not a bitter laughter. The chief comic theme of W. C. Fields, who will seem just as funny in 2000 as he did in 1930, was that of pomposity deflated. His characterization was that of a man having a vast suspicion of society, and protecting himself against a hostile world by a kind of fraudulent truculence and parade of injured dignity. The grandiose air was palpably phony; his comic situations were usually studies in frustration. But you smiled *with* Fields, sympathetically. You always wanted him to come out on top; you were somewhere aware, around the edges, of the pity of life, the futility, the lost hopes. As S. N. Behrman put it: "The comic intuition gets to the heart of a human situation with a precision and a velocity unattainable in any other way."

9

Are Americans "Civilized"?

THE survey we have just concluded has often emphasized *things* in their relation to everyday life,
for so much of what has affected us in the twentieth century
has sprung from technology. It is more difficult to assess
the states of mind of the people who inhabit this world of
things. But American civilization has qualities and boun-
daries not marked by the machine, or even by machine-
produced products for the mind. It might be well, in
conclusion, to examine our own civilization as it has been
appraised by thoughtful critics and to try to see if Americans
are "civilized" in any deeper sense than that which applies
to prosperity, production, gadgets.

There are many commentators who question whether we
are really civilized in this sense. They are so vocal and even
so plausible that one begins to wonder, after reading them,
whether those who are proud of our way of life are living
in a fool's paradise. Some of the criticism is palpably grotesque; if we were to accept it at face value we should have
to rewrite the inscription on the Statue of Liberty to agree
with the one over the gateway to Dante's Inferno: "Abandon
hope, all ye who enter here!" But some of the criticism is

so true, coming from those who wish us well, that it should make us uneasy. Part of the trouble is that we know Americans *mean* well, and this assurance makes us baffled and wistful when we find that many of those who ought to love us, fear us, and are dubious not merely of what we say and do but of what we *are*. Some of this can be written off to ignorance, some to mere envy, but there remains a residue which we have to face up to. Just what *is* the quality of our civilization today?

By "civilization" I don't mean of course our military power, our richness of natural resources, or our technical and industrial know-how—although some of our strength and some of our weakness can be traced to these roots. Civilization, I take it, is a sort of subjective quality, which makes a person or a nation *worthy* of love, respect, admiration. It depends not upon what you have but what you are. Fundamentally it is to be judged by the codes of values which you hold and practice. In this sense "civilization" can be called "culture," in its broad not its narrow meaning. As we look at the United States from this point of view we see a civilization so huge, so complex, so contradictory at many points that none of the oversimplifications which we so often hear, pro or con, will give us the right answer.

Not long ago a professor in the University of Malaya (a reasonably remote spot) announced a lecture. The title was "American Culture: Does It Exist?" This expresses the doubts of many people from other lands who have looked at us and talked about us in print. Their attitudes range as widely as does the accuracy of their information—from the friendly to the puzzled to the contemptuous. In general their indictments run as follows (and I express them in their stronger form): our culture is fiercely materialistic; our only purpose in life is to get money and use it for purposes of power. With an eye always on the main chance, our business and our politics alike have become unscrupulous rackets. We are sordid go-getters; we vulgarize everything we touch. We are belligerent and impetuous in world affairs. We are hypocrites at home and abroad, pretending to certain ways of life and practicing the opposite. We are cocky and immature. Socially we are frightened conformists. We have no arts worthy of the name. The London *Economist* summed up what seemed to its editors the infantile essence of our culture when it said that our influence abroad has been in terms of Coca-Cola, cigarettes, slang, snack bars, roadside advertising, refrigerators, jazz, and movies.

If foreign observers are dubious about our civilization, many of our critics at home seem to be no less so. After World War I some of our more sensitive souls fled from the specter of what seemed to them our bankrupt society and set up in Europe as the Lost Generation, the self-declared expatriates. Most of them crept back home, later on, to a civilization which, whatever its defects, seemed a little better by comparison than Hitler's Europe of the nineteen-thirties.

World War II did not result in a like exodus to Europe; our spiritual expatriates stayed at home this time. Much of the criticism they have directed against American ways of life has been sober and responsible, not cynical. It is the result of a deep love of country and a concern lest we fail to measure up to our opportunities. They look at our civilization with a jaundiced eye but they would like to be helpful and therapeutic about it. In temper and tone the extreme would be represented, I suppose, by the intemperate Philip Wylie, who some years ago in his *Generation of Vipers* withered furiously, with a fine eloquent invective, American sex, American religion, American politics, the American family. The common man, declared Wylie, is narrow-minded, greedy, superstitious, self-seeking, mean, cruel, grasping, insolent.

Almost as severe, with a more limited objective, was the psychoanalyst Robert Lindner, who wrote his book *Must You Conform?* to show that pressures toward conformity are the central danger to American society: that religion, education, philosophy, social work, recreation, are all infused with the rot-producing idea that the salvation of the individual and of society depends upon conformity and adjustment—the sort of conformist that the sociologist David Riesman has called, more calmly, the "other-directed" individual, whose sensitivity to the social group around him is like an antenna to guide his conduct. Along with these we get such a thoughtful critic as Louis Kronenberger, who has documented beautifully his belief that ours *is* an age of vulgarization, that everything is touched up or watered down; that we are naïve and shallow and materialistic; that the two key figures of our tormented age are the press agent and the psychoanalyst. And such a critic as Joseph Wood Krutch believes that as a nation our ethical and philosophical standards are so distorted, so perverted by a mistaken belief in science as God, that our civilization is in a good way to go down the drain.

Many of these critics devote the last page or so of their books to some such pensive consideration as "It may not yet be too late," but for the most part they are pessimistic. Maybe it's the job of intellectuals to worry; certainly they serve a healthy function, and we need as many of them as we can get. The points some of them make about the weaknesses and sterilities of our culture are telling points. But before we decide to jump off the cliff or put the pistol to our head, let's look at the whole thing afresh, without preconceptions, if possible.

Certainly the correct defense against despair of our culture is not to go to the other extreme and join those who are clearly anti-intellectual; those who smugly extol everything we have or are, who ride the crest of an unrealistic optimism and say we are great and happy because we produce more than the rest of the world and therefore have the luxuries which our advanced technology makes possible. Those are the people for whom the phrase "the American Way of Life" means: everything's jake as it is; just join me in sitting on the lid, and keep saying "hitch your wagon to a star"; "paddle your own canoe"; "God helps those who help themselves"—implying a reverence for God as long as He votes *my* party ticket!

Let's try to get a balance.

I suppose the dominant philosophy of Americans ever since they started to hew a country out of the backwoods has been a pragmatic one; a practical one, in which the correctness of values is determined by their practical consequences. "Praise the Lord, but keep your powder dry." We are typically committed to action rather than to reflective thought. We may not be creative of ideas but we know how to put ideas to work. This has resulted in our success in creating an industrial civilization beyond compare. I would submit that there is nothing wrong in this in itself, or in a certain kind of standardization it results in. What's wrong with everyone's having plumbing and bathtubs and electric refrigerators and automobiles? Some Europeans would imply that we are spiritually inferior because we like central heating and garbage grinders, though it should be noted that most of them are remarkably facile in adapting themselves to a higher standard of living when it comes their way. Nor is standardization of certain areas of living always a bad thing. The elevation of my thoughts is not reduced because someone conceived the idea of the interchangeable part. My spiritual life is just as secure as it would be if steel bolts didn't have right-hand threads or if oatmeal still came in barrels instead of cardboard packages.

No, our so-called materialism, insofar as it means merely

more comforts in life for more people, can be easily defended. This is not what our better critics really mean, however. They mean a devotion to material things as the *chief good in life,* success or failure being measured by acquiring or not acquiring them, until the "pursuit of happiness" becomes a pursuit of material things. To the extent that this is true the charges are reasonable. We must control our machine age and subdue it to our own higher interests or we may ourselves become indistinguishable from the machine. But the complexities of American character are such that our susceptibility to material gain is counterbalanced by an idealism just as strong, if sometimes also a little naïve. Our friendly foreign critics have noted that however eager we are to make money, we are just as eager to give it away. Any world disaster finds Americans writing checks to relieve distress. And since the war we have seen the spectacle of the United States sending billions and billions of dollars' worth of goods to countries less fortunate than we. Write some of it off, if you will, to a desire to buy political sympathy; there is still an overplus of goodwill strictly and uniquely American. Generosity and materialism run side by side.

There are, however, other dangers of standardization. Electric refrigerators are one thing and the American mind is another. We have always prized our individualism, but we live under pressures which tend to destroy that and substitute for it a dangerous conformity. By this I don't mean a mere monotony of manners and taste, though that could be very dull indeed. I mean rather the deeper conformities of opinions and attitudes and ideas. Education plays an important part here, for better or worse, and education ought to teach us that there are times when an intelligent dissent is more important than assuming the protective intellectual colorings of one's immediate environment. It is important, however, to know what you are rebelling against and not to become simply another "angry young man."

We have been told frequently, and with some point, that the mass media of entertainment are insidious social forces at work in the land, that here is the vulgarization of culture, standardization at its lowest common denominator. Some of the statistics cited earlier about our national reading habits would support this point of view. And there's not much use in trying to deny that these are weaknesses in our civilization, as we have defined civilization.

It is, however, worth looking for hopeful symptoms in our patient with the fevered cultural brow. The United States has been described recently as being in some respects on the verge of a cultural explosion (though one has to look the other way when the "vast wasteland" of TV is mentioned). It would seem to be true, in a way, in the visual arts and in music. Art museums have never enjoyed such popularity as today. The attendance at the Metropolitan Museum in New York has risen 200 percent since 1950; 4.5 million people visit it each year. And *Life* smuggles in "The History of Western Civilization" and color reproductions of great art. This may be education by indirection, but if 7 million people buy *Life* each week to see the latest designs in bikinis but stay to look at the Rembrandt reproductions they are being exposed to a cultural virus which might take!

In 1962 some $100 million was spent on classical LP records alone, a jump of nearly 700 percent since 1950. And as of 1962 some 40 million people maintained in our cities 1,252 symphony orchestras, 200 of them solidly professional. Americans listen to over 20,000 live concerts a year. There are 780 performing opera groups in the United States, over 2.5 times as many as ten years ago. Some 21.3

million people play the piano, and a total of 33 million play some musical instrument. School bands and orchestras have doubled in number since World War II; there are 73,000 of them now. And believe it or not, about 1,500 harpsichords will be sold this year! The arts (from weekend painting to listening to Bach in hi-fi) were a $2,500,000,000 business in 1960. It is predicted that it may well reach $7,000,000,000 by the nineteen-seventies. Quantitatively and statistically, at least, the cultural explosion would seem to be at hand.

All this is of course subject to interpretation. Some critics would say that a lot of it is done just because it is the "thing to do." That to play a fiddle off key is not to grasp the deeper meaning of music; that to visit the Metropolitan once a year is not proof of a deep understanding of the arts. That to buy a book is not to read it. But few people buy a paperbound copy of Shakespeare in order to impress their friends with it, and harpsichords are not sold for living-room decoration. Not everyone who writes a sonnet or paints a picture is a hidden Shakespeare or Michelangelo or even an Eisenhower, but the mere process of trying to create is likely to make one understand better the superior creations of others. Let's not discourage folk singing because it isn't Verdi.

Self-criticism is a good thing but we should not ignore symptoms of health when they appear. We find much to condemn, much that we should like to see improved—and much that is good. We are a complex and contradictory nation; we bulge in the wrong places, and when we try to glamorize ourselves our intellectual girdles don't always do us justice. We are slaves to conformity but we love diversity. There is no one American way of life. Vermont is not California, nor Illinois Arizona. Even our literature of revolt which emphasizes the bitter and the decadent is a kind

243

of inverted idealism, an implied search for something better. As a whole, we do have values that are not materialistic, though we are frequently inarticulate about them.

Here's the point. Our strength and weakness combine in the democratic experiment which we have chosen as our way of life. Here is our resiliency, our spontaneity, our adaptability, as well as our warmth and friendliness. Here also is our youth and the roughness around our cultural edges. One of the critics most painfully aware of this last is Mr. Dwight Macdonald, one of the liveliest of those who have recently been swinging bludgeons against what seems to them the decay of "high" culture in the United States. He blames this decay on the spread of mass culture, but he is even more alarmed about the growth of what he calls "mid-cult," which he defines as "serious and ambitious work of no quality" which tends to become accepted as "high" culture. This homogenization, he believes, makes indistinguishable the best and the worst, with the result that the cultural and intellectual elite is in danger of disappearing. The middlebrow is Mr. Macdonald's real enemy. Only the few, he argues, are capable of enjoying and understanding the best. If such a former avant-garde artist as Picasso gains acceptance beyond the gates of the elite, then (one assumes) there must be something wrong either with Picasso or the people who like him. (Despite his vigor and wit Mr. Macdonald himself is an admirable writer for the "mid-cult." His pieces often appear in *The New Yorker,* which he himself describes as a "mid-cult" magazine. But Mr. Macdonald is easy to read and enjoy even when you don't agree with him.)

Our more supercilious intellectuals are unconcerned that their "high" culture reaches very few people. It is true that a democratic culture is always of necessity a *popular* culture, and hence dangerously liable to the pitfalls of mediocrity.

But you can't easily have it both ways. Whatever its deficiencies, the great strength and hope for improvement of a democratic culture lies in freedom to change and develop and experiment.

One of the calmest and friendliest foreign observers who wrote about the American scene was the late André Siegfried. In his book *America at Mid-Century* he was a little rueful because he saw us as developing a civilization of our own, with less contact than we should have with the classical tradition of Greco-Latin culture. He was right in believing that Americans could do with a little less action and a little more contemplation, but he granted on the other hand that American civilization has moved toward a new and important concept of human dignity. He saw America, not Europe, as the future center of Western civilization, and he closed his book with the words of the French poet Corneille: "A great destiny is ending; a great destiny is beginning."

It is not difficult to have an affirmative faith in what it is possible for Americans to become.

AND SO ON—A POSTSCRIPT

If you trace the curve of everyday life in America from the mid-sixties into the seventies, several startling things happen. From one point of view it was just more of the same—bigger and better, unless you happened to be one of the 6 percent of the working population which was unemployed in 1971 or were one of the unhappy GI's still slugging out a strange undeclared war in the jungles of Southeast Asia. From another point of view American civilization, within a few short years, was in the throes of a change so rapid, so dislocating, so confusing that many people were fearful as well as puzzled, and our institutions—business, commercial, educational, political, and social—were still trying to adapt to emergencies that no one would have predicted ten years earlier. This chapter can do little more than indicate some of the changes in process.

To begin with: a panorama of some of the more everyday changes. More people were getting themselves born. The 1970 census showed a population of 205 million, a growth of 26 million since 1960. A larger proportion of these people were living in cities and towns; in 1960 there were 15 million people on farms, in 1970, only 10 million. Today 70 percent of the nation's population lives on 1 percent of the land. The trend is alarming because it reflects a depleted and depressed countryside and more congested, problem-ridden cities. The same 1970 census showed that 1 in 15 of our houses and apartments (42.3 million) were with "basic plumbing facilities."

More people were watching television, and perhaps enjoying it less, since a good part of each year was preempted by reruns, and the general quality of entertainment programming seemed to be more imitative and stereotyped than ever. . . . Larger crowds were watching professional football—13 million in 1970, to say nothing of those millions who watched it on TV, in seasons that extended, with pre-and-post-season games, for six months of the year.

There were more people on the move than ever. Some 8

million cars continued to be sold annually. About 80 percent of all United States families now own at least one car and about 30 percent two or more (compared with 16 percent in 1960). At the same time the bicycle population has been growing so fast that it makes the cycling craze of the early 1900's seem small-time. Some 8 million bicycles were sold in the United States in 1971 (half of them for adults). Railroad passenger traffic continued to fall off; there were fewer trains, and few people seemed to want to ride them unless they had to. On the other hand, air traffic grew enormously: in 1963 commercial planes flew 50 billion passenger miles, in 1970, 140 billion miles. Because it was getting cheaper to fly, particularly in groups, Europe was more heavily inundated each year by American tourists. More people were seeing America, too. The facilities of our national parks were so stretched that handling the crowds became a severe problem for the Park Service. Yosemite Park had to ban automobiles from parts of the valley floor because of traffic confusion and smog! And each year saw more and more trailers and campers on the road. Some 320,000 "mobile homes" were built in 1969 as against 150,000 in 1963. More than five million people now live in such homes.*

Not everyone was on the road all the time, however. People still read books and magazines. Twenty-four thousand titles of new books were published in 1970, and the circulation of the *Reader's Digest* climbed to 17,586,000 in 1970. But there were some strange deaths in the magazine field—owing to increased costs and to the loss of advertising, chiefly to TV. The *Saturday Evening Post* stopped publication in 1969, and *Look* magazine in 1971, although it had some 7 million subscribers!

*There were some strange paradoxes here. In a decade culminating in recession and unemployment, more Americans than ever (including blacks) seemed to have more of the comforts and even the luxuries of everyday life and to enjoy a higher standard of living despite inflation. There were not only more automobiles; in 1971 color TV sets were in 1 out of every 3 homes—compared with 1 out of 6 six years earlier. The families with electric dishwashers more than tripled in the past decade, as did those with air conditioners. It was noted, too, that the average family now has five radios to listen to!

The books which were most popular give a clue to one of the major cultural revolutions of our time: the complete relaxation of censorship and the abundance of explicit descriptions of every conceivable kind of sexual activity. The books which can now be bought in paperback at the corner drugstore would have had to be smuggled past customs if they had been imported not so many years ago. Among the ten best sellers in 1970–71 were Philip Roth's *Portnoy's Complaint,* "Penelope Ashe's" *Naked Came the Stranger,* Jacqueline Susan's *The Love Machine,* David Reuben's *Everything You Always Wanted to Know About Sex,* "J's" *The Sensuous Woman,* "M's" *The Sensuous Man,* and Masters and Johnson's *Human Sexual Inquiry.* Confused officials and jurists found themselves unable to define "pornography," and the result was an exploitation of the world of sex which made the eighteenth-century *Memoirs* of "Fanny Hill" seem like high literature.

Good books were still being bought and read, to be sure, by some 15 million Americans. During the late sixties and early seventies there was a spectacular rise in the number of titles on sociology, economics, history, and literature. There were some 2,000 history titles published in 1970, as compared with less than 1,000 in 1960. Psychology and philosophy rose from 300 to 1,200 in the same period; books of technology from 700 to 1,200. Literary titles rose from 750 to more than 3,000.

The new freedom resulted, too, in a kind of movie which escaped entirely from the conventional restrictions which had been laid on Hollywood in earlier days. I am not speaking now of the use of four-letter words (which surfaced even in such old-time stodgy magazines as *Atlantic* and *Harper's*) or of the frankly pornographic "skin flicks" which run openly in some theaters, but of the liberties now available to the "serious" movie with an "X" (adult only) rating. Nude scenes and explicit love scenes, of greater or less subtlety, became almost obligatory in many contemporary movies. Sometimes the scenes added a sensitive artistic value; sometimes they were simply there for their shock value.

And the movies, like TV, suffered from an excess of violence. Even the humor reflected the violence of the times. Movies like *M*A*S*H* and *Catch-22* were a "black humor" reflection of the insanities of war, where things are so horrible that satiric laughter seems the only recourse. Many modern movies string along in a purposefully aimless way, avoiding any semblance of plot. There are no heroes anymore, just antiheroes, and the old-fashioned Hollywood star has pretty well disappeared before a flood of new faces. There are few "happy endings" and often a deliberate avoidance of any sentiment except what can be seen in the overtly physical. The hollowness of the old "dream factory" Hollywood has disappeared (except perhaps for the late movies on TV), to be replaced by a new realism that sometimes shades into a cynicism which is equally hollow. The "drug" scene, the "hippie" scene, the "rock" scene have all been exploited.

Along with all this, some good movies have been made, chiefly by non-Hollywood independent producers working on much smaller budgets than in the old days. As a whole, they reflect the more sensational aspects of our times, which seem to many people to be not the best of all times.

The new frankness applied to stage plays, as well as to motion pictures. The first shocker (it seems tame now) was *Hair*. Later *Oh! Calcutta!* was a highly successful arrangement of self-consciously dirty stories acted out. Another play which had a long run was *The Dirtiest Show in Town,* which the *New Yorker* called "a somewhat inflated claim."

In general, the theater of Arthur Miller and even Tennessee Williams seemed old-fashioned in the late sixties and seventies. The Broadway shows for tired businessmen turned more and more to musicals and to machine-made comedies. Off-Broadway, the "theater of involvement" arose, in which the audience was invited to become involved in the stories of race riots and angry denunciations of the Establishment and to enjoy being insulted by the revolutionary actors on the stage. There is plenty of emotion here, of a very confusing quality.

One learns that his responses can be dulled by the sensational just as his hearing can be dulled, literally, by the convulsive, high-decibel pounding of rock music. That which had shock value at first becomes, at last, simply tedious—whether in art, drama, or literature. Perhaps our salvation lies in the kind of monotony inherent in these many attacks on our senses. It is difficult to feel liberated when one is bored or numbed. We cannot always live in headlines, and we return gratefully to the everyday life which surrounds us.

Perhaps in reaction against the obsession with everything "mod"— clothes, customs, life-styles, literature, theater — there arose in many quarters, in the late sixties and early seventies, a nostalgic return to the past. Nostalgia even became fashionable. It occurred in print: Many thousands of people bought and pored over reprints of old Sears, Roebuck catalogs of the early nineteen-hundreds, thus absorbing a social history of everyday life that many of the readers had never known, but which, at this distance, somehow seemed refreshingly uncomplicated. One publisher even reprinted the 1929 *World Almanac*. Reprints of the long-since-departed *Liberty* magazine and the more recently dead *Saturday Evening Post* were popular. The escape to the past was reflected in other media. Even college students crowded into revivals of *Howdy Doody*. There were Buster Keaton festivals, Chaplin festivals, William S. Hart and Mack Sennett and W. C. Fields and Laurel and Hardy festivals—all of them reaching back to a humor which had not forgotten to be funny.

Two of the big hits on Broadway in the early seventies were *Follies,* a musical which took off from the old Ziegfeld spectacles of the early 'teens and twenties, and *No, No, Nanette,* a revival in which the indestructible Ruby Keeler tap-danced her way through "Tea for Two" and "I Want to Be Happy." People did want to be happy, and were searching, a little wistfully, for a kind of lost world.

Boredom and escape, however, were not the main facts of life in the late sixties and early seventies.

Americans were faced with a financial recession accompanied by a steadily growing inflation—a combination unheard of in past depressions. In 1971 6 percent of our employable population was unemployed, and more than 14 million people were on welfare. The race problem, which had seemed on its way to improvement under Supreme Court decisions, deteriorated into bitterness and violence, chiefly in Northern cities. The slow thrust toward integration was resisted by some black leaders who advocated separateness, rooted in black pride. One can understand their despair and frustration, even if their solution was not likely to be a long-term one.

Crime grew to frightening proportions. Between 1960 and 1969, with the population up 13 percent, the crime rate had risen 120 percent. Many citizens were afraid to walk their own familiar streets. Side by side with this had been a series of terrifying and senseless assassinations, beginning with that of President Kennedy in 1963. Martin Luther King was shot in 1968, Robert F. Kennedy later in the same year. Bombings of banks and schools became frequent items in the news, and it seemed that few of the culprits were ever caught. The use of drugs, both hard and less hard, became a national menace, growing into a scandal even in our armed forces abroad. Protest against social injustices escalated into confrontations, and confrontations into violence of the most reckless kind. Some students in colleges and universities, blamed for their listlessness only a decade before, began to use the machinery of protest, and we had the Kent State and Jackson State disasters. "Hippies" emerged as part of the cultural scene, and the hippies (whose long hair, beards, and granny dresses became, before long, conventional symbols of revolt) were self-consciously "turned off" from society. Many fled to the seeming Nirvana of their communes; frequently they were rebellious members of our best middle-class families, withdrawing into a declared alienation from a social order they reprehended (but upon which, curiously enough, they still in part depended).

American institutions were being questioned and attacked by people some of whom would rather destroy those institutions than try to improve them. Universities, unaccustomed to dealing with violence and unnegotiable demands, floundered helplessly even while admitting that some of the demands for reform were reasonable. But "relevance," the catchword of the student revolt, usually meant the jettisoning of history and any accumulated wisdom of the past and a focus only upon immediate social problems, as if all such problems had been born in the nineteen-sixties.

This partial decay of what had seemed our civilization was aggravated by another very real crisis: the recognition at long last that in all our richness and in all our technological superiority (in large part *because* of our technologized industrialization), we were polluting the land in which we live until it was in process of becoming a desert. Indeed it was worse than that: an active hazard to human life. Air, water, and land pollution, pollution by atomic wastes—all our past negligences rose up to smite us, and we faced the prospect of being choked and poisoned by the products and byproducts of our own vast industrial capabilities. Los Angeles and New York and many other cities were victims of rank atmospheric pollution; even the papers in idyllic Honolulu ran daily counts of the dangerous particles in the air. Lake Erie was becoming an irretrievable sump, and many of our rivers ran foul with chemical refuse.

The overwhelming fact of life, however, was the distant war in Vietnam. The long-time American participation in this conflict began to accelerate in 1965, until finally 400,000 of our military forces were engaged overseas in an attempt to subdue some Southeast Asians. They puzzled us by refusing to be defeated by our massive use of airpower and artillery. The origins of our involvement were obscure, and the reasons for the protection of our "American interest" became increasingly dim. We were somehow "against Communism" and were presumably fighting to ensure "free elections" for a people who had never known free elections. They achieved them, with American help, only in the massively ironic spectacle of 1971, when the single name on the uncontested ballot was that of their "leader," Nguyen Van Thieu.

By this time some 50,000 Americans had been killed, and even the so-called hawks began to wonder how much of our national interest was involved in what had by then become a widened Southeast Asian war in an exhausted, corrupted land. So the United States began to wind down what had been felt by many to be an immoral engagement on our part. Our troops were progressively withdrawn, in terms of a curious official logic which proposed that trained South Vietnamese troops would now be able to win a war which the most powerful nation in the world had been unable to end successfully.

This not only was the most unpopular war in American history, but was also at the root of much of the social unrest which seized the country. Peace demonstrations, marches, confrontations grew in number and intensity—in Washington, in our cities, in colleges and universities, at our political conventions—and, predictably, escalated into bombings and a kind of general destructiveness. This was a violence which no honest citizen could approve of, but it became a tragic part of the total scene of violence. This is not to say that the dissatisfaction with our institutions expressed by many American young people would not have arisen anyway (much of that dissatisfaction was felt by responsible, nonviolent youths), but undoubtedly the war intensified and fed the whole revolt. It was a time, incidentally, when the problems of the young—the so-called generation gap and the search for identity—got more attention in all kinds of books, magazines, and mass media than anyone would have believed possible (except perhaps the young themselves).

This is a strange kind of everyday life I have been describing so far. Is it indeed "everyday" life? It deals with events and attitudes alien to this book as originally written. And if one thinks only of the usual daily round of routines, of family and business and social involvments, it is not "everyday" in the experience of most of us. Even when the conflicts have been most intense, they have involved the active participation of a relatively small number of people. There are more blacks hoping for a quiet, if more rapidly evolving, social justice than there are those who shoot judges in courtrooms. There are more young people in our schools and colleges who still believe in individual responsibility and who are hopeful about what America can mean to them than there are those self-righteous ones who bomb libraries and smash windows or those who "cop out."

But it is clear, I think, that the extraordinary events leading into the seventies *have* become a part of our everyday life in a deep psychological way. What touches us is no longer only our happy acceptance of technological benefits, our reading and our songs, our entertainments and our holidays, or even just our working and eating and sleeping. In a way never felt before, we have become a part of the disturbing incidents, the social miscarriages, and the various kinds of violence which surround us. Everyday things, in a strange way, seem to be more and more identified with the future of the human race. Even our happier and more spectacular national accomplishments have become more a part of our immediate experience.

When Neil Armstrong took man's first walk on the moon in 1969, we watched it "live" by means of a technological miracle and suffered with Walter Cronkite until all the astronauts were back safe on earth.

It is reasonable to believe that these changes in what the word "everyday" means to us were in no small part the result of a more gigantic network of communications than we had ever known before. This is particularly true of TV, whose on-the-spot documentary reporting brings the outside world so immediately and implacably into our homes. We have *seen* assassinations as they have taken place; we have watched riots when they were in progress; we have seen students shot down by militia, and police attacked by mobs. And during the peak of the Vietnam War, instead of reading official bulletins, we *saw* the dead and wounded and saw the GI sweating it out in his jungle outpost. The disillusion which has always been a part of all wars, and was at the center of this one, sat with us as we heard the nightly "body counts."

In a true sense these crises are very real; in another sense, because they dominate our attention so fully, they are larger than total reality. We have been told over and over in all kinds of magazines and books not only that we are living in dangerous times, but that as a people we are possessed by fear and despair and cynicism. One Congressman has said that the most dangerous political trend of the present time is the public's deepening doubt that the government's word means anything.

But hopelessness and cynicism have never been a determining part of the American temperament. Everything that has happened in the past decade has not been bad. Perhaps even in our crises—environmental, racial, global—we have come to closer and more honest grips with reality than in the more distant past. If our world seems sometimes too much with us, there is hope that as a nation we are facing it with more maturity. And what is said on page 245 of this book—that America may be moving toward a new and important concept of human dignity—is perhaps as true as ever. In all probability we shall not reach Utopia by 1984, but neither is it likely that we shall be living our everyday lives in the nightmare predicted by George Orwell's novel.

Index of Proper Names